In Search of Julien Hudson

Free Artist of Color in Pre–Civil War New Orleans

In Search of Julien Hudson
Free Artist of Color in Pre–Civil War New Orleans

WITH ESSAYS BY
WILLIAM KEYSE RUDOLPH
AND PATRICIA BRADY

EDITED AND WITH AN INTRODUCTION BY
ERIN GREENWALD

PUBLISHED ON THE OCCASION OF THE EXHIBITION
In Search of Julien Hudson: Free Artist of Color in Pre–Civil War New Orleans

THE HISTORIC NEW ORLEANS COLLECTION
New Orleans, Louisiana
January 20–April 20, 2011

GIBBES MUSEUM OF ART
Charleston, South Carolina
July 22–October 16, 2011

WORCESTER ART MUSEUM
Worcester, Massachusetts
December 10, 2011–March 11, 2012

PUBLISHED BY
The Historic New Orleans Collection

The Historic New Orleans Collection is a museum, research center, and publisher dedicated to the study and preservation of the history and culture of New Orleans and the Gulf South region. The Collection is operated by the Kemper and Leila Williams Foundation, a Louisiana nonprofit corporation.

Library of Congress Cataloging-in-Publication Data

In search of Julien Hudson : free artist of color in pre–Civil War New Orleans / with essays by William Keyse Rudolph and Patricia Brady ; edited by Erin Greenwald. — 1st ed.
                                 p. cm.
   "Published on the occasion of the exhibition *In Search of Julien Hudson: Free Artist of Color in Pre-Civil War New Orleans.*"
   ISBN 978-0-917860-57-7
   1. Hudson, Julien, fl. 1831–1844—Exhibitions. 2. African American painters—Exhibitions. I. Rudolph, William Keyse. II. Brady, Patricia, 1943– III. Greenwald, Erin. IV. The Historic New Orleans Collection.
   ND237.H865A4 2011
   759.13—dc22

2010022213

First edition. 2,000 copies
All rights reserved
Printed by Imago

Priscilla Lawrence, Executive Director
Jessica Dorman, Director of Publications
Erin Greenwald, Editor

Book design by Alison Cody
New Orleans, Louisiana

Printed and bound in Malaysia for Imago

Jacket Illustration: *Portrait of a Man, Called a Self-Portrait* [detail] by Julien Hudson; 1839, oil on canvas; *courtesy of the Collections of Louisiana State Museum*

Endpapers: *The Cathedral of New Orleans/La Cathédrale* [detail] by Jules Lion; 1842, lithograph; *The Historic New Orleans Collection, bequest of Richard Koch, 1971.32*

CONTENTS

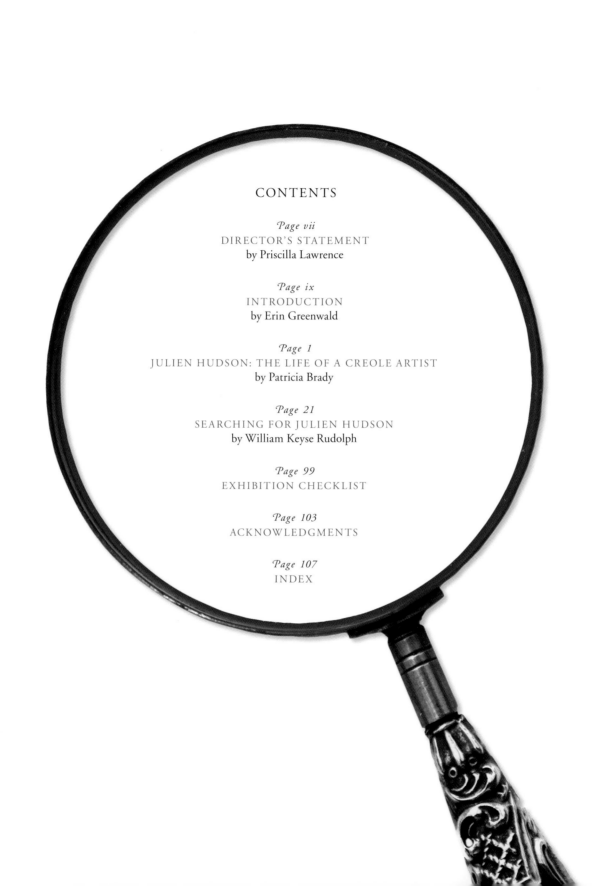

DIRECTOR'S STATEMENT

The Historic New Orleans Collection is proud to present *In Search of Julien Hudson: Free Artist of Color in Pre–Civil War New Orleans*, this fourth in our Louisiana Artists Biography Series. Through collaboration with the Worcester Art Museum, Worcester, Massachusetts, both the book and an exhibition have become a reality.

Julien Hudson is to date only the second-earliest known portraitist of African heritage to have worked in the United States before the Civil War. This initiative has brought together rare and culturally important works by Hudson, as well as a number of portraits attributed to him by style and subject matter. Included both in the book and the exhibition are works by Hudson's teachers and unattributed portraits that reveal the milieu in which Hudson was painting in the first half of the nineteenth century. Our story explores the extraordinary heritage of the *gens de couleur libres*, or free people of color, in New Orleans and across Louisiana.

We are grateful to the director of the Worcester Art Museum, James Welu, and curator of American art, William Rudolph, as well as to all the lenders, both public and private, that believed in the project and provided support. We are also pleased to include the Gibbes Museum of Art in Charleston, South Carolina, as one of the three exhibition venues for *In Search of Julien Hudson*. Through its membership, the Laussat Society of The Historic New Orleans Collection has made possible the publication of this and all of our artist biographies. We offer our sincere thanks.

— Priscilla Lawrence, *Executive Director*
THE HISTORIC NEW ORLEANS COLLECTION

INTRODUCTION

Recovering the past—or at least a version of the past as stitched together by historians, genealogists, curators, and the like—is a daunting task that requires patience, persistence, and more than a small dose of imagination. Imagination, in the framework of historical inquiry, should be equated not with fabrication but rather with the inquirer's ability to fashion a story out of the disparate facts surrounding a moment in time. In the quest to recover the story of a single individual, context—the historical environment of time and place—is everything.

Julien Hudson, student and teacher, artist and free man of color, was a product of a very specific time and place: pre–Civil War New Orleans. He was a French-speaking Catholic raised primarily by women in a city where his racial ancestry and status as a free person of color left him forever straddling the line between those who enjoyed the full freedoms and protections of the law and those who most assuredly did not.

At the time of Hudson's 1811 birth, the city's population stood at just over 17,200 souls. The territory of Orleans had not yet become the state of Louisiana. Sail-powered vessels were still the most frequently sighted ships at the port of New Orleans, and the War of 1812—the culmination of a decades-long effort to establish American economic and commercial independence—was not yet underway. But over the course of the next three decades of Hudson's life, the city and its inhabitants would undergo one of the most transformative periods in their history.

Between 1810 and 1840, New Orleans emerged as the steam-powered-transportation hub of the South. Increased opportunities attracted tens of thousands of newcomers from the eastern seaboard

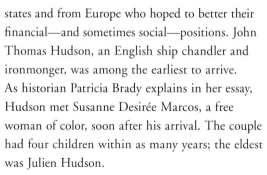

states and from Europe who hoped to better their financial—and sometimes social—positions. John Thomas Hudson, an English ship chandler and ironmonger, was among the earliest to arrive. As historian Patricia Brady explains in her essay, Hudson met Susanne Desirée Marcos, a free woman of color, soon after his arrival. The couple had four children within as many years; the eldest was Julien Hudson.

By 1830 the trickle of European immigration from France, Germany, and Ireland, in particular, had become a stream, by 1840 a river. The existing population grew apace, especially within the city's community of free people of color. Their ranks more than doubled by the time a fifteen-year-old Julien began his formal artistic training with itinerant Italian miniaturist Antonio Meucci in the mid-1820s.

As members of an intermediate caste with historic ties to both the free white and enslaved populations, free people of color occupied a tenuous position within the city's social, economic, and political hierarchy. In 1830 they constituted 24 percent of the city's nearly 50,000 inhabitants and more than 35 percent of the city's free population. No other urban population in the slaveholding South came close to mirroring New Orleans's demographic. Baltimore's percentage of free people of color was a distant second, at 15 percent. In Louisiana, city and state efforts to reduce the community's numbers and mobility—through residency restrictions, limits on emancipation and manumission, and other bureaucratic measures—met with mixed results.

Julien Hudson's own story, as traced through time and space by art historian William Keyse Rudolph, reveals the striking level of mobility available to some free people—or, more specifically, native-born free men—of color. Two documented trips to Paris, including a mid-1830s voyage that afforded Hudson the opportunity to study with well-known French painter Alexandre-Denis Abel de Pujol, placed him in the company of an elite group of New Orleans–born free men of color. In crossing the geographic divide separating them from France, these men strove to reinforce their ties to the cultural heritage with which they identified. Back in New Orleans, Hudson worked his French connection to his advantage, using what Rudolph describes as a "newly acquired Parisian gloss" to attract prospective clients. But questions remain about the limits placed upon him as a free artist of color operating in an environment in which opportunities for advancement became increasingly circumscribed as the nineteenth century progressed.

Julien Hudson's portrait-painting career was short—he died young, at age thirty-three, in 1844. The circumstances surrounding his death are a mystery. All that remains of his body of work are five paintings by his hand and two attributed to him by stylistic affinity. It is difficult to know whether these works are a reasonable representation of his artistic abilities, but in the context of American art history, their mere existence has fueled a lively discussion about the painter and his world. *In Search of Julien Hudson: Free Artist of Color in Pre–Civil War New Orleans* is the most thorough examination to date of the time and place that shaped, nurtured—and perhaps limited—Julien Hudson's artistic horizons.

— Erin Greenwald, *Editor*
THE HISTORIC NEW ORLEANS COLLECTION

JULIEN HUDSON:
THE LIFE OF A CREOLE ARTIST

by Patricia Brady

Julien Hudson was a professional artist in New Orleans from 1831 through 1844. He was the first native-born portraitist to practice in the city and the second documented painter of African descent in the United States, following Joshua Johnson of Baltimore. Because of the scantiness of the records and small number of extant paintings, Hudson has never received his due in American art history.

A free man of color, Hudson could trace his ancestry back to the days when New Orleans was a struggling military outpost of the French empire, the capital of a largely unsettled wilderness (fig. 1). Hudson's grandmother, Françoise Leclerc, was born in New Orleans around 1752, ten years before the French ceded the colony to their Spanish allies. She and her younger sister Charlotte, both mulattoes, were the daughters of Annette, a black slave of the Leclerc family, and an unknown white man, perhaps Leclerc himself.[1] As a teenager, Françoise caught the eye of François Raguet, an unmarried merchant. He was a member of the French Superior Council, the judicial branch of the French colonial government, which maintained oversight of the colony during the transition from French to Spanish governance. Raguet (then aged forty-seven) bought Françoise (then aged seventeen) in 1769. The act of sale contained a condition requiring Raguet to free Françoise after six years of servitude, but Raguet did not wait the full six years.

Appearing before New Orleans notary Andrés de Almonéster y Roxas in 1772, Raguet presented a copy of the 1769 agreement. At this time he freely remitted the remaining years

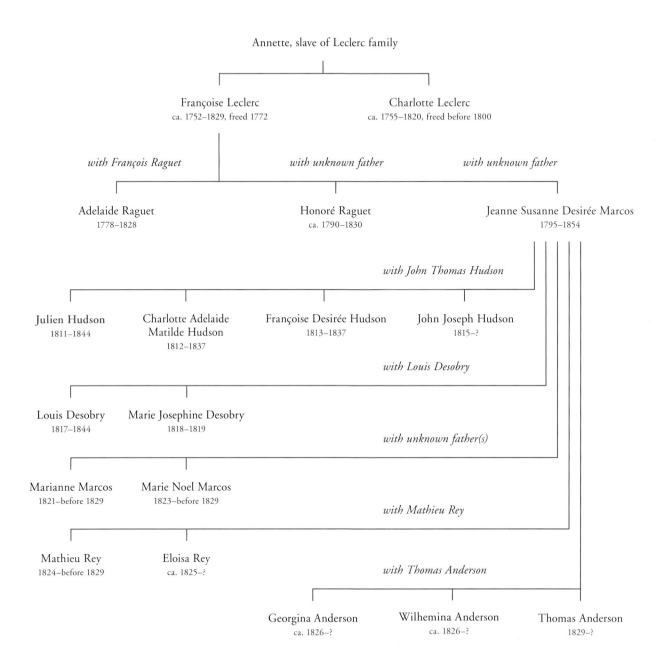

Figure 1

FAMILY OF A CREOLE ARTIST

of her servitude.[2] Clearly, he was enamored of the young woman. Françoise Leclerc and François Raguet continued their relationship for some years after he granted her freedom.

In April 1776, Françoise, likely with financial support from Raguet, purchased a four-bay Creole cottage on Bienville Street, one door down from Bourbon Street.[3] Like many unmarried women in the city, she set aside part of the house as the family residence and rented the extra rooms as a source of regular income. Two years after she purchased the house on Bienville, Françoise gave birth to Adelaide Raguet, whom François Raguet recognized as his natural daughter in 1782. At the same time that he acknowledged paternity, Raguet provided for Adelaide's future maintenance with the donation of two slaves and two city lots on Conti Street, only three blocks from Françoise's Bienville Street house.[4] The acts of donation were carefully constructed so that the property was safe from any possible counterclaims, and he affirmed the great love and affection he felt for both mother and daughter. Françoise gave birth to another child, Honoré Raguet, around 1790. Despite Honoré's surname, the identity of his father is unclear.

When Françoise was nearly forty, she chose her own lover, another white man, with whom she had a quadroon daughter on August 11, 1795—Jeanne Susanne Desirée Marcos, always called Desirée.[5] Nothing is known of Desirée's father except his probable surname, Marcos, and his race, although Creole naming patterns, in which the first-born child is often named for the father, suggest that his first name may have been Jean.

Desirée's birth and baptism were recorded in the baptismal register of the St. Louis Cathedral (fig. 2). Baptism was a major event in the lives of Creoles, of color or otherwise, and the role of godparents usually fell to other family members, including white relatives. Married or not, free women of color often gave children their fathers' surnames, and Catholic priests recorded them, making their lineage clear.

In the summer of 1803, Desirée's eighth year, word of events taking place across the Atlantic reached the ears of New Orleans's citizenry. A shocked populace learned that France—the nation that only months before had reestablished sovereignty over the colony—had sold the entire Louisiana territory, including New Orleans, to the United States. This news was especially unsettling for free Creoles of color. Life under both the French and Spanish regimes had provided them with many advantages and safeguards. Here, and in other French and Spanish colonies, free people of mixed race were considered a third caste, neither white nor black—unlike in the United States and British colonies, where white was white and black was black, with any racial mixture being perforce black. Members of the free colored community in New Orleans enjoyed many of the rights of whites: They could own property, enter legal contracts, sue and be sued, marry legally (though not to whites), testify in court, inherit and donate property, study and teach, work in many capacities, and even become rich.

But the United States regarded people with any African ancestry as black and subject to the legal restrictions imposed by individual cities or states. Even though some northern states had begun

Figure 2
THE CATHEDRAL OF NEW ORLEANS / LA CATHÉDRALE
by Jules Lion
1842, lithograph
The Historic New Orleans Collection, bequest of Richard Koch, 1971.32

a process of gradual emancipation after the American Revolution, slavery—and restrictions on employment, franchise, marriage, and residency for free blacks—remained realities throughout the United States and its territories. Worse yet were the southern states, which would soon include Louisiana. The economic and social elite in the South depended on plantation agriculture and its expansion into new areas; tight control of an enslaved black work force was essential to maintaining the plantation system. One essential justification for slave labor was the entrenched belief that blacks were inherently inferior to whites. Free people of color, particularly when they were successful, were seen in the South as a dangerous anomaly, liable to create unrest and jeopardize the institution of slavery itself.

In the decade following the Louisiana Purchase, however, most rights enjoyed by free people of color in the territory seemed secure, even if the local economy did not. Privileges granted by earlier governments were not easily abrogated. Free Creoles of color in New Orleans retained most privileges, their status, and an open social familiarity with whites unheard of in the rest of the nation.[6] And as matriarch of her own family, Françoise Leclerc continued to reign supreme, regardless of the changes taking place in the city. Within three blocks of her house lived her eldest daughter, Adelaide Raguet, as well as her sister Charlotte Leclerc, now also freed and working as a seamstress.[7] Honoré and Desirée still lived at home, but it was Desirée who was the child of Françoise's heart. Françoise tried hard to care for her younger daughter since she had neither the inherited advantages of Adelaide nor the gender advantages of Honoré, who could support himself through any number of trades.[8] In the eighteenth and early nineteenth centuries, the education of girls of any race or class was usually catch as catch can. Françoise was illiterate, but determined to do better by Desirée. There is no evidence to indicate where she studied, but the young girl was clearly educated, as she wrote with a beautiful, flowing hand. Desirée became an unusually independent woman, charting her own course in life. She was fiercely protective of her children, financially savvy, and willing to go to court to protect her interests.[9]

The years after the Louisiana Purchase were an economic disaster for New Orleans, but Françoise Leclerc managed to get by, continuing to rent out rooms in her house to maintain a steady income. The British and French had recommenced their hostilities—now royalist Britain against Napoleonic France. The United States, its interests, and its sovereignty were of no account to the European combatants. American ships were seized, cargoes confiscated, and sailors impressed. In 1807 President Thomas Jefferson imposed a two-year embargo on international trade to avoid being drawn into the raging war, shutting down the port. New Orleans was in the doldrums. All its residents in businesses that depended on the port, including wholesalers, bar owners, and landladies, saw their incomes plummet.

Despite the stagnant business environment, John Thomas Hudson, a native of London, came to New Orleans in the early 1800s to set up shop. He was first listed as a merchant in 1809; from a building on South Levee Street, which faced the river, Hudson advertised as an ironmonger and ship chandler. He apparently lived and conducted business in the same building, along with two young men who may have been clerks or other employees.[10] At some point Hudson encountered Desirée Marcos. They began a relationship in 1810, when she was fifteen. Throughout the War of 1812, they were a couple.

Racism and draconian laws against interracial marriage limited the marital options open to Creoles of color. The nineteenth-century stereotype, made famous by male travelers from outside Louisiana and later mythologized by white Creole historian Charles Gayarré, was that mixed-race women of New Orleans were available to any white man with enough money to support them in style. At the quadroon balls or elsewhere, according to these tales, a woman's mother would bargain for a financial arrangement called *plaçage* through which a white lover took care of her and any children, providing a house and financial support when the man left the relationship to marry a white woman. The woman might then form a liaison with another white man or marry a free man of color. According to such accounts, mixed-race women always preferred white men to men of their own caste. Of course, the women themselves didn't publish accounts of their true preferences, and their actions, recorded in marriage records and notarial acts, indicate a far more complex story.

Like most stereotypes, however, there were morsels of truth embedded in the popular stories. Certainly some women of mixed race entered into liaisons with a series of white men. Narratives of these women come from travelers who, almost to a man, attended a quadroon ball while in the city; they sought no information about free women of color who led different sorts of lives. Writers accepted the self-serving and often degrading opinions of local white men. One local planter, hoping to enlighten French writer Alexis de Tocqueville, stated: "At New Orleans there is a class of women dedicated to concubinage. They are the coloured women. Immorality is for them in some sort a professional duty which they perform faithfully. A coloured girl is destined from her birth to be a white man's mistress."[11]

Marriage, however, was the preferred and most prestigious choice for mixed-race women. By the end of the eighteenth century, there were many educated, financially successful free men of color who were legally free to marry their female counterparts. Probably the second choice for free women of color was committed cohabitation with a white man. From the late 1700s through the 1830s, scholar Gregory Osborn has found more than 500 mixed couples, prevented from marrying legally, who nevertheless formed lifelong relationships with an emphasis on family stability, care for children, and financial continuity.[12] The family lives of other native-born Creole artists who might be considered Julien Hudson's contemporaries—Florville Foy, Eugène Warburg, and Louis Lucien Pessou—conformed to those norms. All three had supportive fathers—a Frenchman, a German, and a Creole of color from St. Domingue—who were committed to or married to their mothers, saw to their sons' educations, and provided financial support for their careers.[13]

Hudson was the exception. His mother Desirée had relationships with at least six white men over forty-five years, never settling on a lifetime companion. Unlike the mothers of the other noted Creole artists, Desirée fit the stereotype of the quadroon who lived monogamously with a series of white lovers.

Julien Hudson, the first child of the union between Desirée Marcos and John Hudson, was born January 9, 1811, and baptized August 8 of that year. His sisters, Charlotte Adelaide and Françoise Desirée, followed in March 1812 and November 1813, respectively. A final child—a boy christened Joseph, but later called John—was born in February 1815, a month after the American victory at the Battle of New Orleans.[14]

No further Hudson children were born, and John Hudson himself disappeared from the city directories by 1822. After a brief boom at the end of the war, New Orleans slumped again into recession. It is likely that Hudson returned to England, seeking better business opportunities. Throughout their relationship, Desirée and the children, and perhaps John Hudson, had lived in part of her mother's house on Bienville Street. On October 19, 1816, Desirée bought the small house next door.[15] It is possible that she had received a settlement from John to care for their four children.

After Hudson's departure, Desirée lived with Louis Desobry, a native of Cap Français, St. Domingue. A white refugee from the Haitian Revolution, Desobry was part of a wave of French-speaking immigrants whose arrival in the first decade of the nineteenth century helped maintain French culture and language in New Orleans for many years after the Louisiana Purchase. The couple had a son, Louis, in May 1817 and a girl a year later, who died before her second birthday.[16] Desobry soon afterward left the city—and Desirée—to become a planter in Iberville Parish, where he married a white woman and had a legitimate son (also named Louis).

In the 1820s, the city's stagnant economy suddenly took off as Anglo-Americans and newly arrived Europeans inundated the city, seeking their fortunes. Since the landing of the first steamboat at New Orleans in 1812, increasingly larger and more powerful vessels had chugged up and down the Mississippi and its tributaries, following the Ohio River as far north as Pittsburgh. The populous new states of the Midwest and South that lay along the river were major agricultural export producers and markets for imported goods. Located near the mouth of the Mississippi, New Orleans was the entrepôt of the Gulf Coast, receiving both raw materials from upriver and manufactures from the northern states and Europe. By 1830, it could truly be called a city, spreading both downriver and upriver as suburbs (*faubourgs*) developed. It was a prosperous time for businesses—and by extension, landladies—in New Orleans.

Desirée Marcos lived with at least two other white men, Mathieu Rey and Thomas Anderson, in the 1820s and gave birth to seven more children, the last in 1829.[17] During these years, Desirée's eldest child Julien received a good basic education. Perhaps his mother taught him and his siblings herself. Or perhaps he attended one of the small private schools so common in the city. Some local Creole men or French immigrants—never white Americans—taught a few Creole boys at their houses. Judging by the results, these teachers were more than competent. At thirteen, Julien's early education was considered complete, and it was time to fit him for a profession.

On November 22, 1824, Desirée signed an agreement of indenture for Julien with a local tailor (fig. 3). She, Julien, and the tailor, a free man of color named Erasme Legoaster, appeared before

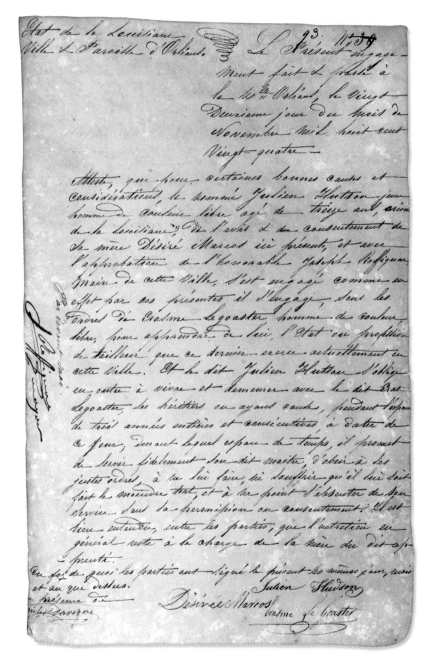

Figure 3
INDENTURE CONTRACT
November 22, 1824
courtesy of the Louisiana Division, City Archives of the New Orleans Public Library

Mayor Joseph Roffignac. Beginning that day, the boy would live at Legoaster's house, which encompassed his shop, for the next three years. Legoaster would teach him the craft of tailoring, while Julien agreed to work faithfully and obey his master.[18]

Apparently tailoring did not agree with him. A year before finishing his indenture, the fifteen-year-old Hudson left Legoaster and decided to become a portrait painter. But why? There were no other professional artists in the family, nor other obvious influences in that direction, and tailoring was a steadier and more profitable trade than painting. Whatever its origin, the desire to study painting coincided with the November 1826 reappearance of Roman miniaturist Antonio Meucci, who had worked in the city some years earlier. An artist who defined "peripatetic" (setting up studios everywhere from Salem, Massachusetts, to Cartagena, Colombia, and points in between), Meucci was a man of many talents. He painted miniature portraits, retouched damaged works, executed new opera scenery and house decorations at the Orleans Theatre (fig. 4), and ran a drawing and painting school out of his rooms on the corner of Royal and St. Peter streets, only five blocks from Julien's house. The few months Hudson studied with Meucci must have been extraordinary for the aspiring artist, and he must have acted quickly to secure lessons, because Meucci's last local advertisement appeared in May 1827; by 1828 he was in Havana, Cuba.[19]

Painting portraits was what Hudson loved and what he would do for the rest of his life, profitable or not. Evidence suggests that Julien went to live with his grandmother when he left

ORLEANS THEATRE.

Figure 4
VIEW OF ORLEANS THEATRE [DETAIL]
ca. 1845, engraving
The Historic New Orleans Collection, 1974.25.36.90

Françoise Leclerc. L'an mil huit cent vingt neuf, le cinquante troisième de l'indépendance des États Unis, le dix huit avril, à dix heures du matin, moi Théodore Seghers, notaire public, commissionné pour la ville et paroisse de la Nouvelle Orléans, État de la Louisiane y demeurant, je me suis transporté d'après réquisition au domicile de Françoise Leclerc, femme de couleur et libre, rue Bienville, dans une maison qui m'a été dite lui appartenir, où étant, j'ai trouvé la dite Françoise Leclerc malade et alitée, mais ayant toute sa mémoire et son intelligence ainsi qu'il apparaît avec évidence à moi notaire et aux trois témoins soussignés. Laquelle voulant faire des dispositions testamentaires m'a requis de les recevoir en présence des trois témoins soussignés, et elle me les a dictées comme suit et je les ai écrites telles qu'elle me les a dictées, le tout en présence de Mess. François Castelneau, Jean Piquegny et Louis Germain Sassinot, domiciliés tous trois en cette ville, témoins, à ce requis, lequel testament est de la teneur suivante.

Je me nomme Françoise Leclerc, enfant naturelle d'Annette Leclerc, je suis âgée de près de quatrevingts ans, & née en ce pays, je n'ai point été mariée.

Je lègue & donne ma négresse Frosine âgée de trente cinq ans à ma fille Désirée Marcos, en récompense de toutes les peines & de tous les soins qu'elle a eus de moi depuis ma maladie.

Je lègue à ma petite fille Mathilde Hudson, fille de Désirée Marcos mon petit nègre Félix âgé de huit ans, je fais présent et donation à ma petite fille Désirée Hudson sœur de la précédente du petit nègre Louis âgé de quatre ans, je donne à John Hudson mon petit fils que j'aime par prédilection, enfant de Désirée Marcos, les deux négresses Marie âgée de vingt cinq ans environ & Marguerite de quatorze ans, je donne et lègue cent gourdes à Pickit Hudson, frère du précédent. Je donne aussi cent gourdes à Eloisa Ray, ma petite fille & fille de Désirée Marcos, je donne & lègue également cent gourdes à chacun de mes petits enfants, Wilhelmine Anderson, Louis Desoby & Georgina Anderson. ils auront tous droit à ces legs aussitôt après mon décès, je fais tous ces legs aux enfants de ma fille tant à cause de l'amitié & de l'affection qu'elle m'a toujours montrées depuis que nous sommes ensemble que par ce qu'elle est dans l'indigence & n'aurait nul moyen de se soutenir. Je n'ai jamais fait de testament antérieurement à celui ci.

Et la testatrice déclarant n'avoir plus rien à mentionner aux présentes, moi notaire soussigné, je lui ai donné lecture des présentes à haute & intelligible voix en présence des dits témoins, et en leur présence la testatrice a déclaré le bien entendre, le bien comprendre & y reconnaître ses dernières intentions dans lesquelles elle persiste. Dont acte.

Fait et clos de suite, sans interruption & sans divertir à d'autres actes au domicile susmentionné. Et la testatrice interpellée de signer, a dit ne le pouvoir ne sachant écrire et a fait sa marque, le tout en présence des dits témoins qui ont signé avec le notaire soussigné.

Legoaster's house to study with Meucci.[20] Although she had tenants, Françoise's house was larger than his mother's; and his mother's small house must have been crowded with children, making concentration difficult. At thirty-four, Desirée had recently changed her allegiance from Mathieu Rey to Thomas Anderson. There were four older children living in the house—the teenaged girls, Charlotte and Desirée Hudson, and the somewhat younger boys John Hudson and Louis Desobry, eleven and nine—as well as toddlers and babies.

Many aspects of Julien Hudson's career remain shrouded in mystery. But a will made by Françoise Leclerc (fig. 5) on April 18, 1829—along with the subsequent inventory of her property— was the Rosetta stone that unlocked some secrets of Hudson's personal life and complicated web of family relationships. The will also includes the first known reference to Julien as "Pickil" (fig. 6).[21]

Like many people of the day, Françoise waited to make her will until she was dying. Her most valuable property was her house on Bienville Street, which contained furniture, personal belongings, and a little table silver, and another old house, presumably one she rented out, in the next block. She also owned three adult black slave women, Marguerite, Frosine, and Marie (who was listed as "an African"), as well as Frosine's two little boys, and an eleven-year-old mulatto called Aspasie.[22]

In her bequests, she willed Frosine to her daughter Desirée "in recompense of all the troubles and all the cares that she has had from me since my sickness." Then to her granddaughters Charlotte and Desirée Hudson, she gave Frosine's two little boys; to John Hudson, her godson and favorite grandson, she left the other two adult women. To Desirée's remaining children, she left 100 gourds each.[23] As the dying woman explained it, she made these legacies to her daughter's children "because of the friendship and affection which she has always shown me since we have been together," as well as out of fear that Desirée might fall into indigence and be unable to support herself. The will was read aloud to Françoise, and she agreed that it incorporated her intentions, duly making her mark in the presence of the notary Theodore Seghers and three witnesses.[24]

After Françoise died, her property was inventoried on June 3 and 5, 1829. The appraisers, Jean Rousseau and Louis Hazeur, were free men of color.[25] After the individual bequests were fulfilled, her property was divided into thirds—one part to Desirée Marcos, one part to Honoré Raguet, and the final part to Adelaide Raguet's four surviving children.[26] Adelaide herself had died the previous year, leaving her children as joint heirs to her portion of the estate.[27]

The inventory showed that Françoise occupied a bedroom at the front of the house, a kitchen (also containing a bed), pantry, hall, gallery (probably at the back), and the backyard. All other rooms in the house were rented. It seems likely that Julien lived with Françoise because he claimed two bedsteads in the front room as his own property during the inventory. In a large mahogany armoire in that room, besides clothing and papers, the appraisers found two paintings. These may have been Hudson's student work, given the improbability of his grandmother having purchased any paintings of her own. Perhaps he had spent the two years since Meucci's departure honing his skills.

The appraisal for the entire estate was $6,849.25, a respectable amount for the time.[28] Desirée bought the remaining slave and her mother's house from the other heirs in August 1829, likely with the aid of Thomas Anderson.[29] Her family moved into the larger dwelling, while she retained ownership of her own house next door, probably as rental property.[30]

The chronology of Julien Hudson's next two years is unclear, like so much else concerning the artist. How he occupied himself from the time of his grandmother's death in 1829 until he placed his first advertisement in the New Orleans *Bee/l'Abeille* on June 6, 1831, is unknown. When he first offered his services "to the ladies and gentlemen of New Orleans" as a miniaturist and drawing teacher, he described himself as a pupil of Antonio Meucci, "having lately gone through a complete course of studies."[31] He again advertised as a painter in December 1831, this time in the *Louisiana Courier/Courrier de la Louisiane*, where he added the information that he had "lately returned from Paris." That ad continued to run through the next month. His studio address was 117 Bienville, his mother's house. She had given up a room, perhaps the front bedroom that opened on the street, for her son's atelier.[32]

In New Orleans, the economic boom of the previous decade continued. An earlier description of the city as "a thoroughfare of speculators, and brief sojourners, going and coming, whence and where, few know, and few care" was truer than ever.[33] Since Hudson's birth, the resident population had climbed from 17,242 in 1810 to 46,082 in 1830.[34] New Orleans had become one of America's largest cities. In fall and winter, the Mississippi levee was lined for miles with huge ocean-going sailing ships, their tall tree-like masts visible from a distance, and steamboats, "in doubling files, prow to stern, and broadside to broadside."[35] They were hemmed in by innumerable flatboats, keelboats, barges, rafts, and market boats.

As the city had changed, so too had life on Bienville Street. Desirée and Thomas Anderson had parted company. Desirée's eldest daughter Charlotte Hudson had married Belsince (or Belsunce) Louis Liautaud, a free man of color, and moved into a home of her own. More change came in 1837: Julien left for Paris, this time to study with the well-known artist Alexandre-Denis Abel de Pujol. Desirée, while Julien was abroad, sold her mother's house for $10,000 and moved back to her own house next door.[36] In February, Charlotte died, shortly before her twenty-fifth birthday.[37] And in November, Françoise (also known as Desirée) Hudson died, too.[38]

Besides family problems, the Panic of 1837—a severe economic downturn that began in New York City in May of that year—brought an end to Julien's foreign studies. Within a month, the national economy fell into a depression that lasted for the next five years. New Orleans was especially hard hit with bank closings, a sharp decline in international trade, and numerous business failures. When Julien returned from Paris in August, he returned to a bleak economy. Although he is listed in the 1837 and 1838 city directories as a portrait painter residing at 120 Bienville, it is doubtful that he found many patrons.[39] The matriarchs of the family were gone, and now Julien had only his mother and surviving siblings for comfort.

Only three portraits survive from this later period; whether he painted others that were lost or destroyed is unknown. At this time, Hudson also taught at least one student, George David Coulon (fig. 7), a French-born white New Orleanian, who went on to a successful career as a portraitist and landscape painter. Late in life Coulon wrote an autobiographical letter for his friend and fellow artist Bror Anders Wikstrom, listing all the artists he had known in New Orleans. This letter makes clear that Hudson was Coulon's teacher.[40]

If the facts of Hudson's career are hard to ferret out, the facts surrounding his death are an almost total mystery. Coulon recorded the date of his teacher's death (1844), which provided a starting point for research. But no obituary, death certificate (fig. 8), or interment record has been found for Julien Hudson in 1844, when he would have been thirty-three. Coulon, however, was not in error. Indices of

Figure 7
GEORGE DAVID COULON
by Eugène Simon, photographer
ca. 1895, photoprint
The Historic New Orleans Collection, 1981.109

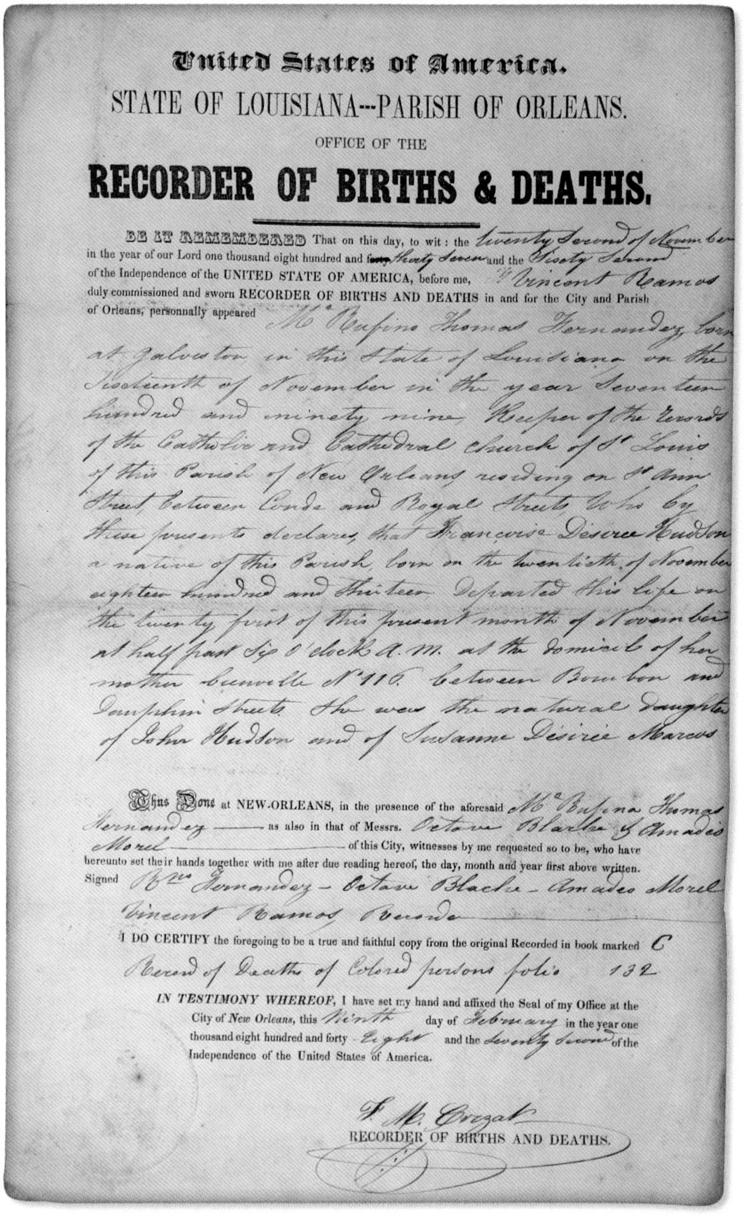

United States of America.

STATE OF LOUISIANA--PARISH OF ORLEANS.

OFFICE OF THE

RECORDER OF BIRTHS & DEATHS.

BE IT REMEMBERED That on this day, to wit: the twenty Second of November in the year of our Lord one thousand eight hundred and ~~four~~ thirty Seven and the Sixty Second of the Independence of the UNITED STATE OF AMERICA, before me, Vincent Ramos duly commissioned and sworn RECORDER OF BIRTHS AND DEATHS in and for the City and Parish of Orleans, personnally appeared Mr Rufino Thomas Fernandez born at Galveston in this State of Louisiana on the Sixteenth of November in the year Seventeen hundred and ninety nine, Keeper of the records of the Catholic and Cathedral church of St Louis of this Parish of New Orleans residing on St Ann Street between Conde and Royal Streets who by these presents declares, that Françoise Desiree Hudson a native of this Parish, born on the twentieth of November eighteen hundred and thirteen departed this life on the twenty first of this present month of November at half past Six o'clock A.M. at the domicil of her mother Bienville No 116. between Bourbon and Dauphin Streets. She was the natural daughter of John Hudson and of Susanne Désirée Marcos

Thus Done at NEW-ORLEANS, in the presence of the aforesaid Mr Rufino Thomas Fernandez —— as also in that of Messrs. Octave Blache & Amadée Morel —— of this City, witnesses by me requested so to be, who have hereunto set their hands together with me after due reading hereof, the day, month and year first above written.

Signed Rno Fernandez - Octave Blache - Amadeo Morel
Vincent Ramos Recorder

I DO CERTIFY the foregoing to be a true and faithful copy from the original Recorded in book marked C Record of Deaths of Colored persons folio 132

IN TESTIMONY WHEREOF, I have set my hand and affixed the Seal of my Office at the City of New Orleans, this Ninth day of February in the year one thousand eight hundred and forty - Eight and the Seventy Second of the Independence of the United States of America.

F. M. Crozat
RECORDER OF BIRTHS AND DEATHS.

Figure 8

DEATH CERTIFICATE OF FRANÇOISE DESIRÉE HUDSON

November 22, 1837

courtesy of the Louisiana Division, City Archives of the New Orleans Public Library

For Julien Hudson, no death certificate, like this one for his sister Françoise Désirée Hudson, was ever recorded.

court records show that the artist did indeed die that year, preceded in death by his half brother Louis Desobry.[41]

In August 1844 "Julien alias Pickel" Hudson filed his half brother's succession, but the document is missing from the district court files.[42] In a perhaps connected event, Desirée Marcos sold her remaining Bienville Street property on August 28, 1844, and moved downriver to Barracks Street.[43] Subsequently, she filed the succession of her son Pickil Hudson, who died in December 1844.[44] That document is also missing. Thanks to Françoise Leclerc's will, we know that Julien Hudson was known as Pickil Hudson by his family. Both documents were likely removed by the clerk of court at a later date and attached to a subsequent court case, making them all but impossible to find.

The lack of a listing in the death records for 1844, though, is a lead of another sort. Unnatural deaths—suspected homicides and suicides—were not listed in the regular death register. Instead, they came under the purview of the coroner and were brought by him before a coroner's jury that determined the cause of death. If Julien Hudson met an untimely end that year, the circumstances are unknown. The coroner's records for 1844 are incomplete; the extant records begin February 19 and end August 1, with no mention of a Hudson. Perhaps, giving in to despair, Julien Hudson took his own life in December 1844, a terrible disgrace in Catholic New Orleans. Like most of the details of the artist's life, this is mere supposition—sustained, whether justifiably or not, by the memories of subsequent generations.

Julien Hudson's life is a striking example of the way true stories mutate and assume mythical qualities over time. Rodolphe Lucien Desdunes (1849–1928), the son of free people of color who had emigrated from St. Domingue in the early nineteenth century, was a member of the same community as Hudson. Cigar makers by trade, the Desdunes family also included poets and writers among their number. Rodolphe Desdunes followed the family trade at first, but after the Civil War he became active in Republican politics, working for many years for the United States Customs Service. He was a tireless advocate for civil rights, joining forces with such leaders as Homer (Homère) Plessy, Paul Trevigne, and Aristide Mary. He wrote for Dr. Louis Martinet's *Crusader* and self-published pamphlets on topics of political and social interest to African Americans.

The crowning interest of his life, and the work for which he is best known, is a small volume of reminiscences and oral history that he labored over for many years. He was indefatigable in bringing together information about free people of color and their descendants that otherwise might have been forgotten or lost. Writing in his native French, he memorialized them in *Nos hommes et notre histoire (Our People and Our History)* (fig. 9).[45]

In this work he brought together information about the men and a few women of his community who made names for themselves in business, politics, the arts, religion, philanthropy,

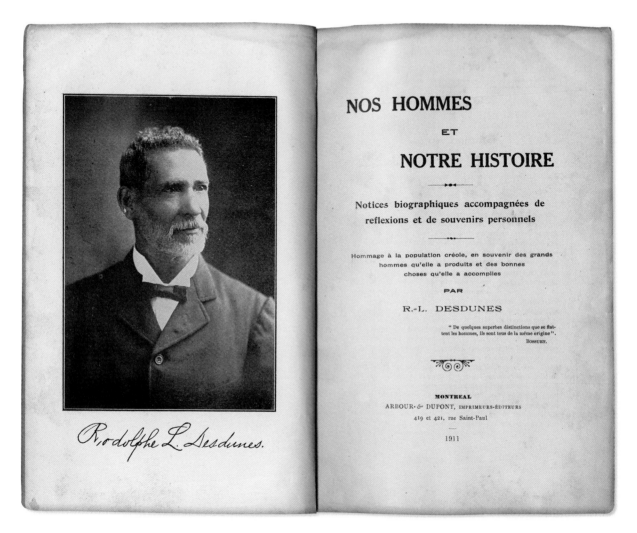

Figure 9
NOS HOMMES ET NOTRE HISTOIRE
by Rodolphe Lucien Desdunes
Montreal: Arbour & Dupont, 1911
The Historic New Orleans Collection, 69-201-LP.5

and other areas. Besides his own experience of Reconstruction and the Jim Crow era, he drew heavily on early communal memories. Born five years after Hudson's death, Desdunes still heard echoes from the previous generation of the Creole painter who had finally despaired of recognition. The man's name was "Pickhil," and Desdunes somehow came up with "Alexandre Pickhil." No such person appears in any record, civil or religious. Clearly the person he wrote about was Julien "Pickil" Hudson.

Listen to his words:

We had our Titian in Louisiana in the person of Alexandre Pickhil. We know that Pickhil produced magnificent pictures, but he has left us nothing as a legacy, perhaps because he became disillusioned. He is said to have executed a full-length portrait of an eminent ecclesiastic, but he destroyed this masterpiece because of vicious criticism passed upon it. Thus, although Pickhil may have been the best painter of his era, he preferred to die in misery and anonymity rather than display his talent to the detriment of his self-respect. He died in New Orleans about the middle of the past century, between 1840 and 1850. It is said that disillusionment cast a cloud of despair over his whole life.[46]

Desdunes may have gotten the name wrong, but the sentiment was true. Julien Hudson was a pioneering artist of color who attempted to succeed in a white world where the odds were stacked against him. His struggle, his achievements, and the paintings he left behind are a celebration of the human spirit and a tribute to the Creoles of color of nineteenth-century New Orleans.

NOTES

1   In the French and the Spanish colonies, degrees of whiteness and blackness in mixed-race people were considered important parts of the public record and usually appeared in legal documents. The designations used were *metif* or *metis* (indicating mixed African and Indian parentage or ancestry), *mulatto* (half black, half white), *quadroon* (one-quarter black), and *octoroon* or *tierceron* (one-eighth black); as time passed, and the number of those with only the slightest trace of African ancestry increased, the latter terms were frequently stretched to include them. For a recent discussion of race labels used in eighteenth- and early-nineteenth-century Louisiana, see Jennifer Spear, *Race, Sex, and Social Order in Early New Orleans* (Baltimore: Johns Hopkins University Press, 2009), 14–16, 97–98, 181–82.

2   Acts of Andrés de Almonéster y Roxas, 11 February 1772, no. 35, New Orleans Notarial Archives (hereafter NONA).

3   Acts of Juan B. Garic, 30 April 1776, vol. 7, no. 130, NONA; Vieux Carré Survey (hereafter VCS), square 68, The Historic New Orleans Collection (hereafter THNOC).

4   Acts of Leonardo Mazange, 18 March 1782, no. 283v–287v, NONA. Intriguingly, the donated property adjoined the house of a free black woman, Naneta alias Leclerc. Naneta is a plausible variant of Annette. Perhaps this woman was Françoise's mother, freed by Monsieur Leclerc and provided with a house and slaves. Six months later, she made her will as Magdalena Naneta (probably Madeleine Annette) Leclerc, freeing two of her three slaves and directing that her money be used to free her slave husband. Acts of Mazange, 3 October 1782, no. 833, NONA.

5   Baptism of Jeanne Susanne Desirée Marcos, Saint Louis Cathedral (hereafter SLC), B 13, 264, Archdiocesan Archives of New Orleans (hereafter AANO).

6   As the nineteenth century progressed, Louisiana's free people of color experienced a gradual erosion of their rights that culminated with a series of laws passed by the state legislature intended to restrict the growth of the free colored caste and limit the intrastate movement of the preexisting population. See, for example, Richard Tansey, "Out-of-State Free Blacks in Late Antebellum New Orleans," *Louisiana History* 22 (1981): 369–86 and Shirley Elizabeth Thompson, *Exiles at Home: The Struggle to Become American in Creole New Orleans* (Cambridge: Harvard University Press, 2009), 81–82, 114–15.

7   VCS, square 97, THNOC; New Orleans City Directory (hereafter NOCD) 1809, 1811, 1822, 1823, 1827.

8   When François Raguet died in 1802, he left Adelaide 3,000 pesos. To her sons he left 1,000 pesos each; to his eldest granddaughter he left a plantation and twelve slaves. No such provisions were made for Honoré and Desirée, though Raguet did leave 400 pesos to Françoise Leclerc. Acts of Pedro Pedesclaux, 18 November 1802, no. 849, NONA.

9   See, for example, Desirée Marcos v. Louis Desobry, 3 May 1819, Orleans Parish Court, docket no. 2405, New Orleans Public Library (hereafter NOPL).

10   NOCD 1809, 1811; 1810 U.S. Census, Orleans Parish, Territory of Orleans.

11   "Conversation with Mr. Brown … a distinguished lawyer and a rich planter from Louisiana," 28 October 1831, in Alexis de Tocqueville, *Journey to America*, ed. J. P. Mayer, trans. George Lawrence (New Haven, CT: Yale University Press, 1959), 71.

12   Information courtesy of Gregory Osborn of the Louisiana Division of NOPL, an authority on the history and genealogy of free people of color in New Orleans. For several years, Osborn has collected information on committed interracial relationships; he plans a publication in the near future.

13   Patricia Brady, "A Mixed Palette: Free Artists of Color of Antebellum New Orleans," *International Review of African American Art* 12, no. 3 (1995): 6.

14   Despite the efforts of several researchers, the baptismal record of Julien Hudson was not found until the 1990s. The priest officiating, Father Kouny, mistakenly wrote that he had baptized a *girl*, Juliana, the child of a free woman of color named Susana Desirée Marcos. No father was named at the time. The baptismal records for his sisters, however, make it clear that this was indeed a mistake made by the priest and that the baby was a male, Julien Hudson. Baptism of Julien Hudson, SLC B 24, 79; Baptism of Charlotte Adelaide Matilde Hudson, SLC B 25, 81; Baptism of Françoise Desirée Hudson, SLC B 27, 34; and Baptism of John Joseph Hudson, SLC B 28, 104, AANO.

15   Acts of Marc Lafitte, 19 October 1816, vol. 9, no. 448, NONA.

16   Baptism of Louis Desobry, SLC B 30, 85; Baptism of Marie Josephine Desobry, SLC B 30, 85; Interment of Marie Josephine Desobry, SLC F 12, 3, AANO.

17   Baptism of Mathieu Rey, SLC B 35, 128; Baptism of Marianne Marcos, SLC B 32, 132; Baptism of Marie Noel Marcos, SLC B 34, 112; Baptism of Thomas Anderson, SLC B 42, 12, AANO. For three additional children of Desirée Marcos not found in the sacramental registers, see also Will of Françoise Leclerc, 18 April 1829, filed 29 May 1829, Will Book 4, NOPL.

18   Contract of indenture between Erasme Legoaster and Julien Hudson, 22 November 1824, Records of the Mayor's Office, vol. 4: 93, NOPL. Legoaster must have been a family friend; in April that same year, he served as sponsor at the baptism of Desiree Marcos's daughter Marie Noel. See Baptism of Marie Noel Marcos, SLC B 34, 112, AANO.

19   See "Meucci, Anthony," in *Encyclopædia of New Orleans Artists, 1718–1918,* ed. John Mahé II, Rosanne McCaffrey, and Patricia Brady Schmit (New Orleans: The Historic New Orleans Collection, 1987), 261.

20   Inventory of Françoise Leclerc, Acts of Theodore Seghers, 3 and 5 June 1829, vol. 2, no. 250, NONA.

21   Will of Françoise Leclerc, NOPL.

22   Ibid.

23   Ibid. The gourd or *gourde* was the official monetary unit of nineteenth-century, post-independence Haiti. It is unclear why Françoise Leclerc used the unit in her will (though a survey of contemporary New Orleans notarial documents suggests she was not alone in doing so), but specie being scarce, citizens often resorted to whichever currency was available. The present-day equivalent of 100 gourds is approximately $2,400. These bequests to her grandchildren also benefited Desirée since the funds of minor children would have been in her hands, and if any of them died before maturity, she would have been their natural heir.

24   Ibid.

25   Inventory of Françoise Leclerc, NONA.

26   Acts of Seghers, 17 October 1829, vol. 2, no. 427, NONA.

27   Succession and Inventory of Adelaide Raguet, 1828, Orleans Parish Court of Probates, NOPL.

28   Inventory of Françoise Leclerc, NONA.

29   Acts of Seghers, 28 August 1829, vol. 2, no. 394, NONA.

30   VCS, square 68, THNOC.

31   New Orleans *Bee/l'Abeille*, 3 June 1831.

32   *Louisiana Courier/Courrier de la Louisiane*, 3 December 1831, 10 January 1832.

33   Henry Cogswell Knight, *Letters from the South and West* (Boston: Richardson and Lord, 1824), 126.

34   1810 U.S. Census, Orleans Parish, Territory of Orleans and 1830 U.S. Census, Orleans Parish, State of Louisiana.

35   Knight, *Letters from the South and West*, 116.

36   Acts of Felix Grima, 5 January 1837, vol. 13, no. 931, NONA.

37   Charlotte's death was noted in the succession of Desirée Marcos, City of New Orleans, Second District Court, docket no. 8354, NOPL.

38   Succession of Françoise Desirée Hudson, City of New Orleans, First District Court, docket no. 1882, NOPL.

39   NOCD 1837, 1838.

40   George Coulon, "Old Painters of New Orleans," unpublished MS, 1901, 2, Scrapbook 100, Louisiana State Museum.

41   "Desobry, Julien alias Pickel & Louis Desobry, f. p. c." are listed as having filed a succession in P. M. Bertin, *General Index of All Successions Opened in the Parish of Orleans, from the Year 1805, to the Year 1846* (New Orleans: Yeomans & Fitch, 1849), 72.

42   Ibid.

43   Acts of Felix Percy, 28 August 1844, vol. 18, no. 310, NONA.

44   Bertin, *General Index of All Successions*, 110.

45   Rodolphe Lucien Desdunes, *Nos hommes et notre histoire* (Montreal: Arbour & Dupont, 1911). All citations from this source will be taken from the translated edition, *Our People and Our History: Fifty Creole Portraits*, trans. Sister Dorothea Olga McCants (Baton Rouge: Louisiana State University Press, 1973), xiv–xv, xvii, xviii.

46   Ibid., 71.

SEARCHING FOR JULIEN HUDSON

by William Keyse Rudolph

Julien Hudson's story is alluring, frustrating, and poignant. An artist who died young and left a fragmentary body of work, Hudson (1811–1844) offers a path into a unique historical moment in a city that has always provided ample fodder for commentary, invention, fantasy, and fascination. Identified as being a person of color by individuals who could not have known him when he was alive, Hudson was not verified as a person of mixed racial ancestry in the historical record until 1995, after nearly a century in which he was steadily enshrined as one of the earliest artists in the new histories of African American art.[1] His story, in his own life and afterwards, is a combination of detection, speculation, and invention, conducted by researchers, genealogists, and art historians. His artistic reputation rests upon a handful of secure paintings and a group of attributed works. Only one work can be more or less traced from the easel to its current location. Another passed through the hands of Dr. Isaac Monroe Cline, one of Louisiana's most important early art collectors—although Cline made no mention of the artist or painting in his seminal sketch of Louisiana art.[2] And one—and possibly two others—may have intersected with one of the most powerful free families of color in the state. Nothing can definitively be proven about these works or their histories, ensuring that the aura of mystery surrounding them—and their maker—will undoubtedly persist.

Figure 1
MARIANNE CELESTE DRAGON
attributed to the school of José Francisco Xavier de Salazar y Mendoza
ca. 1795, oil on canvas
courtesy of the Collections of Louisiana State Museum, gift of John T. Block, 05750

AN ARTIST'S CAREER

Julien Hudson began his artistic studies as a teenager. His intersection with the visual arts is not surprising. Much evidence exists to suggest that New Orleans's population of free people of color boasted a sizable number of artisans and craftspeople. One in four New Orleans cabinetmakers at the time of Hudson's birth was a free man of color.[3] During Hudson's own career, he was one among many documented free artists of color, from native-born sculptors Eugène (1825 or 1826–1859) and Daniel Warburg (1836–1911), to marble cutter, sculptor, and tomb designer Florville Foy (1820–1903) and French-born photographer and lithographer Jules Lion (ca. 1810–1866).[4]

Free people of color were not only makers of art. Evidence of their patronage of Louisiana's visual culture dates as far back as the Spanish colonial period. One of the oldest extant paintings from colonial Louisiana is the portrait of Marianne Celeste Dragon (fig. 1), attributed to

Figures 2, 3 & 4
PIERRE TOUSSAINT
JULIETTE NOEL TOUSSAINT
EUPHEMIA TOUSSAINT
by Antonio Meucci
ca. 1825, watercolor on ivory
*courtesy of the Collection of
The New-York Historical Society,
1920.4, 1920.5, 1920.6*

Born in St. Domingue, Pierre Toussaint had been brought to New York as a slave around 1787, but earned his freedom after his master Jean Bérard's death by supporting his widowed mistress as one of New York's most successful hairdressers. From Meucci, he commissioned miniatures of himself, his wife Juliette Noel, and his niece Euphemia.

an artist working in the circle of José Francisco Xavier de Salazar y Mendoza (ca. 1750–1802), the earliest documented artist in New Orleans. Although the fact goes unmentioned in the literature surrounding this work, Dragon was a free woman of color, and her race later became the subject of controversy.[5]

Julien Hudson's first art teacher was Antonio Meucci (active 1818–ca. 1850), an itinerant portraitist first recorded in New Orleans in 1818, and then again in 1826–27.[6] Before he took Hudson on as a pupil, Meucci had interacted with free people of color as patrons, suggesting that, as far as payment for services rendered was concerned, he was colorblind. During his New York itinerancy in 1823, he painted three members of the Toussaint family (figs. 2–4).[7] Meucci returned to New Orleans in 1826 to work on decorations for the Orleans Theatre. To supplement his income he advertised his services heavily in local newspapers. It was perhaps through these advertisements that Hudson, then aged fifteen or sixteen, first came in contact with Meucci. By the following year, Meucci and Hudson were teacher and student.[8]

From Meucci, Hudson discovered the techniques of making a miniature. He likely learned how to prepare the surface, usually a thinly sliced disk of ivory, and how to apply watercolors with the controlled, economical movements required of the medium. Miniature painters typically used a small, felt-covered slant-top desk that tilted upwards, bringing the disk close to the painter. Meucci also probably taught Hudson how to execute the final touches necessary to package the finished portrait, including attaching the ivory to a support—often a playing card—and then packing it into a bezel, or frame.[9]

Although he advertised as a portrait as well as a miniature painter, no full-length Meucci portraits are known. What has survived is a fairly large group of miniatures. From these small works in watercolor on ivory, his style can be judged. Two miniatures in particular show a disparity of accomplishment. The artist seems most comfortable working at bust length. His *Portrait of a Gentleman* (fig. 5) gives us a closed-lipped sitter who assuredly dominates his oval setting. Meucci convincingly suggests the textures of various objects, from the unidentified sitter's slightly windblown hair to the translucent edging of his cravat, through which peeks a hint of the navy lapel. Meucci also delightfully endows his sitter with a hint of stubble over his upper lip—hard to read, much less paint, on such a small scale. Yet, for all these talents, the artist had some difficulty in what happened below the shoulders. A hint occurs in *Portrait of a Gentleman*, where the sitter's right arm seems abruptly foreshortened and skinnier than it should be. The portrait of Dona Maria Theresa Piconelle (fig. 6), painted at three-quarter length, further reveals Meucci's difficulty with anatomical drawing. After dwelling on her shining chestnut hair and pleasant face, Meucci seems content to merely delineate her neck, arms, torso, and midsection. Although he pays some attention to modeling in Piconelle's puffed sleeves, her bent right arm, and the folds of her dress, there is no real form underneath the high-waisted gown. For that matter, her head seems slightly too large for her sloping shoulders, while her left arm, continuing down past the viewer's gaze toward the bezel, assumes disturbing proportions.

Figure 5
PORTRAIT OF A GENTLEMAN
by Antonio Meucci
ca. 1825, watercolor on ivory
courtesy of the New Orleans Museum of Art, Museum Purchase, Shirley Latter Kaufmann Fund, 99.63

Figure 6
DONA MARIA THERESA PICONELLE
by Antonio Meucci
ca. 1818, watercolor on ivory
courtesy of the Collections of Louisiana State Museum, 08943.30

Figure 7
GIRL WITH A RATTLE
by Antonio Meucci
ca. 1825, watercolor on ivory
courtesy of a private collection through Elle Shushan

Figure 8
PORTRAIT MINIATURE OF A CREOLE LADY
attributed to Julien Hudson
ca. 1837–39, oil on panel
courtesy of the collection of Laura Schwartz and Arthur Jussel;
photograph by Eric Weiss

As miniaturists, Meucci—and Hudson after him—would not have had the luxury to concentrate on the rich, painterly effects made possible through a build-up of glazes of oil paint, or the careful construction of a figure from an underdrawing on a ground layer that could then be embellished. Hudson would certainly have learned flourish—miniatures lent themselves to that, and Meucci could provide it in discrete areas (fig. 7)—but not the idea that forms are volumes to be filled up through an additive process.

Although Hudson left no signed miniatures, a recently discovered miniature (fig. 8) has been attributed to him, based on its New Orleans provenance and the resemblance of its female sitter's features to those of the male subjects in *Portrait of a Man, Called a Self-Portrait* (fig. 9) and a mid-1830s attribution titled *Portrait of a Creole Gentleman* (fig. 10). The individuals have distinctive

Figure 9
PORTRAIT OF A MAN, CALLED A SELF-PORTRAIT
by Julien Hudson
1839, oil on canvas
courtesy of the Collections of Louisiana State Museum, 07526 B

Figure 10
PORTRAIT OF A CREOLE GENTLEMAN
attributed to Julien Hudson
ca. 1835–37, oil on canvas
courtesy of the Dallas Museum of Art, gift of Curtis E. Ransom

Figure 11
PASCUALA CONCEPCIÓN
MUÑOZ CASTRILLÓN
by Antonio Meucci
ca. 1830, watercolor on ivory
courtesy of Neal Auction Company

physiognomies—long noses, narrow faces, and large eyes—that seem to denote a common artistic conceit, if not an outright familial connection. Beyond the sitters' facial similarities, the clothing in the two male portraits dates from roughly the same time period. What is even more tantalizing than the resemblance is the miniature's composition, which is strikingly similar to a signed work from around 1830 by Antonio Meucci (fig. 11). Although the Meucci portrait is today in a less than ideal state, due to overexposure of its support to light and a trimming of the ivory surface during its history in family collections, the composition is still legible enough to suggest a stylistic relationship to the miniature attributed to Hudson. The female sitters mirror each other's seated posture in front of windows, with marine views beyond. Both hold objects in their laps; both drape lace shawls over their dresses. The Meucci miniature dates from the artist's Colombian period; however, it may be an example of the artist's reusing a prototype he already had employed in New Orleans and that his pupil had seen and emulated. As we will continue to see, provocative artistic and biographical possibilities are easier to suggest than to prove when discussing Hudson's career.

During much of the nineteenth century, France's capital operated as a magnet, drawing elite young free men of color from France's current and former colonies in search of greater educational opportunities than existed at home. New Orleans offered free men of color some opportunities for study, mostly in private schools, such as the Sainte-Barbe Academy, founded by Michel Séligny (who

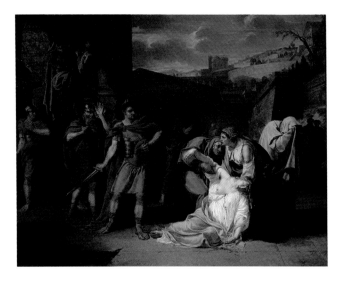

Figure 12
THE DEATH OF CAMILLA
attributed to Guillaume Lethière
1785, oil on canvas
courtesy of the Rhode Island School of Design Museum,
gift of Lucy T. Aldrich, 72.144

Figure 13
GIRL WITH PORTFOLIO
by Guillaume Lethière
ca. 1799, oil on canvas
courtesy of the Worcester Art Museum,
Worcester, Massachusetts, museum purchase, 1954.21

studied first in France), or the school opened in 1813 by G. Dorefeuille.[10] But for the sons of well-to-do free people of color—and, indeed, for their white male counterparts—Paris beckoned.[11] As recounted by Rodolphe Lucien Desdunes, the civil servant, community organizer, and historian who compiled *Nos hommes et notre histoire* (*Our People and Our History*), the voyage to Paris for privileged free men of color became an educational rite of passage.[12] For ambitious young men of color, like the poet and New Orleans native Pierre Dalcour (b. 1813), France was where one "could enjoy freedom and all the advantages that science, literature, and the arts offer to spirits that nourish themselves on such things."[13] The frequency of these study-abroad sojourns increased as many southern legislatures, including Louisiana's, intensified legal efforts to restrict both local and interstate movement of free people of color in the mid-nineteenth century.[14]

The career of Guillaume Lethière (1760–1832) offers a dazzling historical example of the possibilities that an artist of mixed race could achieve in Paris. Born on the island of Guadeloupe, Lethière was the illegitimate son of Marie-Françoise, a freed slave woman also known as Pepeÿe, and Pierre Guillon, a white civil servant of French descent.[15] Lethière followed his father (who did not officially recognize Lethière as his son for another twenty-five years) to Paris at age fourteen. From there the aspiring young artist traveled to Rouen. His early work showed promise, prompting him to return to Paris and enter the highly competitive and politicized world of the Royal Academy. Like his classmates, Lethière came under the pervading influence of neoclassicism (fig. 12). He competed unsuccessfully three times for the Prix de Rome, the three-year fellowship to Italy that was the object of every ambitious young art student's desires. Although he never won the prize, an aristocratic admirer of his work, the Comte de Montmorin, convinced the Academy to arrange an honorary fellowship at the French Academy in Rome as consolation. After his studies in Italy, Lethière acted as emulator of and rival to the great Jacques-Louis David (1748–1825), operating a competing studio in Paris in the 1790s. He also maintained close ties to the Bonaparte family, under whose patronage he worked in Spain and Italy, where he served as director of the French Academy in Rome. Whether painting historical or religious subjects, or engaging in portraiture, his style remained firmly entrenched in the classicizing idiom of his youth, as one of his rare extant portraits reveals (fig. 13).[16]

A career like Lethière's was in part possible because the French, whatever their personal sentiments, did not obsess administratively about the race of ex-colonials coming to study and work there. Although slavery in France was not abolished permanently until 1848, a series of legal decisions in the eighteenth century resulted in a bifurcated system, whereby the institution of slavery remained legal in France's colonies but not in the metropole. Some free men of color were drawn to the country they considered their cultural or ancestral homeland. That the metropole also provided an environment free from the worry of re-enslavement made it doubly attractive.[17]

Yet France's legal openness to people of color does not mean that the study-abroad experience was completely race-neutral. While passenger lists and police records did not note race, prejudice doubtless existed in the real, as opposed to the paper, world. Even

MINITURE PAINTING.

J. HUDSON, lately returned from Paris, begs leave to offer his services to the ladies and gentlemen of New-Orleans, as Miniature Painter. All orders thankfully received and punctually attended to at No. 117 Bienville st.

December 3.

AVIS—S. HUDSON, *PEINTRE EN MINIATURE*, récemment de retour de Paris, prend la liberté d'offrir ses services aux Dames et Messieurs de la Nlle.-Orléans. Il recevra avec reconnaissance tous les ordres qu'on voudra bien lui donner, et les exécutera ponctuellement.

3 déc– *Rue Bienville, No.* 117.

Figure 14
ADVERTISEMENTS FOR JULIEN HUDSON FROM THE ENGLISH AND FRENCH EDITIONS
OF THE *LOUISIANA COURIER/LE COURRIER DE LA LOUISIANE*
December 3, 1831
courtesy of the Louisiana Division, City Archives of the New Orleans Public Library

Lethière, with his long list of honors, hit a stumbling block in his artistic ascent during the Bourbon Restoration that may have been due to his racial heritage as much as his work for the Bonapartes.[18] Nevertheless, in principle, the official mechanisms of cultural education were colorblind. And for those who were light enough in complexion, the absence of official categories of racial documentation meant that many of them passed as white in their day-to-day interactions. Contemporary evidence suggests that Lethière's skin color and features did not immediately mark him as a person of mixed ancestry.[19]

Over fifty years after Lethière first arrived in Paris, so did young Julien Hudson, although the exact dates of his first Parisian trip are unclear. Hudson's grandmother Françoise Leclerc passed away in 1829, leaving Hudson enough money to help fund his first trip to Paris, which seems to have happened sometime between her death and 1831.[20] His address in Paris is unknown, and his studies cannot be verified in the institutional record. He turns up nowhere in the *cadastres,* or tax records. Nor does his name appear in the Institut de France's student registers. The only French document capturing Hudson's presence is an 1831 French passport register, where he is listed as an "American student."[21] It is thus unclear whether he formally pursued an artistic education, obtained a general liberal education, or simply absorbed the sights, sounds, and life of Paris during this visit.

Whatever his actual itinerary, by December 1831 Hudson was back in New Orleans. Besides the additional stylistic affinities of the attributed miniature portrait and the Meucci work, advertisements in local newspapers make clear that Hudson considered himself a miniature painter in the tradition of his master. A June 1831 advertisement named Meucci as an instructor, rather than Alexandre-Denis Abel de Pujol (1785–1861), the French artist with whom he has also been linked historically. A subsequent advertisement (fig. 14), which ran three times between December 3, 1831, and January 10, 1832, promoted Hudson as a miniaturist, even while mentioning his newly acquired Parisian gloss.[22]

But if Hudson began his professional career as a miniaturist, changes to the New Orleans art scene meant that he would soon have to think—and paint—on a larger scale. Within little more than a week of Hudson's latest advertisement, the *Helvetia* landed in New Orleans from Le Havre, France. The ship carried a passenger whose arrival heralded a dramatic influx of European artists to New Orleans. Although transatlantic painters and sculptors had been active in the city for several decades, the arrival of Jean-Joseph Vaudechamp (1790–1864) on January 18, 1832, inaugurated a surge. An ambitious portraitist who had been trained in the Parisian studio of Anne-Louis Girodet-Trioson (1767-1824), one of the epicenters of contemporary French painting, Vaudechamp dominated the art market in New Orleans for most of the decade. His success in the city prompted him to encourage several of his former classmates from Girodet's studio to try their luck in New Orleans, resulting in the residencies of Aimable-Désiré Lansot (1799–1851), François Fleischbein (1801 or 1803–1868), and

Figure 15
MARIE ALTHÉE JOSEPHINE D'AQUIN DE PUÈCH AND ERNEST AUGUSTE DE PUÈCH
by Jean-Joseph Vaudechamp
1832, oil on canvas
The Historic New Orleans Collection, 2005.0340.1

Figure 16
PORTRAIT OF A LITTLE GIRL, CALLED "EUPHROSINE"
by Jean-Joseph Vaudechamp
1836, oil on canvas
courtesy of a private collection

Page 35

Figure 17
CARL KOHN
by Jacques Guillaume Lucien Amans
ca. 1837, oil on canvas
The Historic New Orleans Collection, 2006.0425.1

Jacques Amans (1801–1888), among others. Lansot, Fleischbein, and Amans continued to work in the city long after Vaudechamp's 1839 departure.[23]

These artists brought with them a high degree of technical accomplishment; fine, precise brushstrokes were the norm, with impasto often reserved for areas of detail, such as accessories (figs. 15 and 16). Due in large part to their presence, New Orleans in the 1830s transitioned from a city of miniaturists to a city of easel painters. It is no accident that the largest number of surviving antebellum Louisiana paintings date from the 1830s and '40s. And as the number of trained painters operating in Louisiana increased, so too did the range of sitters' postures depicted in their work (as seen in the Amans portrait of the young Carl Kohn (fig. 17), who leans casually out at the viewer). Hudson would have witnessed this change firsthand. Indeed, he seems to have chosen his next teacher, François Fleischbein, in the hope of making his own transition from miniature to easel.

Franz Joseph Fleischbein was born in Godramstein, a small Bavarian town northwest of Stuttgart, close to the French border. After training in Munich, he made his way to Paris, where he studied with Girodet.[24] A sketchbook, containing studies from the antique and drawings made after Jacques-Louis David's *Oath of the Horatii* (always a touchstone for serious young artists of the late eighteenth and early nineteenth centuries), documents his presence in Paris.[25] By July 1833, Fleischbein was in New Orleans. The following advertisement announced his services:

> *F. Fleischbein, peintre de portraits, nouvellement arrivé de France, a l'honneur de prévenir les habitans de cette ville, qu'il fait des portraits à l'huile et au dessin, en touts grandeurs desirables, dont il garantira la resemblance parfaite. Les personnes qui desireraient examiner ses ouvrages et se faire peindre par lui, peuvent s'adresser à l'Hotel de la Marine, rue de la Levée.*[26]

For ease with his Creole clients, he Gallicized his name, resulting in the curious hybrid "François Joseph Fleischbein" by which he is usually known.[27] Fleischbein was not as technically proficient as his other European colleagues. Nevertheless, he was a charming artist whose talents were best displayed in portraits of female sitters. In a small portrait of his wife, *Marie Louise Têtu, Madame François Fleischbein* (fig. 18), the artist combines French academic style with a certain sweetness and charm intrinsic to German Biedermeier painting. The result testifies to the truly cosmopolitan nature both of the Paris ateliers in the nineteenth century and the New Orleans art scene in the 1830s.

Fleischbein's grounding in traditional techniques is apparent in a rapidly executed preparatory drawing of his wife (fig. 19). Other examples of compositional studies for later, finished works testify to Fleischbein's subscription to the core principle of French art instruction, namely that drawing was the starting point for all art.

That Fleischbein knew the theory but had difficulty with the practice is borne out by his most ambitious paintings: a full-length portrait of an unknown Creole subject (fig. 20), a delightful

Figure 18
MARIE LOUISE TÊTU, MADAME FRANÇOIS FLEISCHBEIN
by François (Franz) Fleischbein
ca. 1833–36, oil on canvas
courtesy of the Dallas Museum of Art, American Painting Fund, and the Patsy Lacy Griffith Collection, gift of Patsy Lacy Griffith

Figure 19
SKETCH OF MARIE LOUISE TÊTU, MADAME FRANÇOIS FLEISCHBEIN
by François (Franz) Fleischbein
before 1833, pen, ink, and chalk
courtesy of the Dallas Museum of Art, American Painting Fund, and the Patsy Lacy Griffith Collection, gift of Patsy Lacy Griffith

Figure 20
PORTRAIT OF A CREOLE LADY
by François (Franz) Fleischbein
ca. 1830s, oil on canvas
courtesy of Matilda Gray Stream

Figure 21
PORTRAIT OF BETSY
by François (Franz) Fleischbein
1837, oil on canvas
The Historic New Orleans Collection, 1985.212

Figure 22
CHILDREN OF
COMTE LOUIS AMEDÉE DE BARJAC
by François (Franz) Fleischbein
ca. 1839, oil on canvas
*courtesy of the Collections of
Louisiana State Museum, 09461*

bust-length portrait of his housekeeper (fig. 21), and a group portrait of the children of Louis Amedée de Barjac (fig. 22). In these paintings, Fleischbein easily establishes rapport between sitter and viewer, providing hints of lively minds behind the often-sideways gazes his sitters level at their audiences. Yet at a certain scale, the artist's difficulty with anatomy becomes manifest, whether in the tiny feet poking out from underneath the Creole woman's voluminous bell skirt, or in the de Barjac children's boneless hands.

Two paintings executed immediately after Hudson's tutelage with Fleischbein show that the young artist took practical examples from the European painter's compositions. His earliest-known easel painting, *Portrait of a Young Girl with a Rose* (fig. 23), adopts the background of Fleischbein's *Marie Louise Têtu* with a low horizon line and generic landscape setting. Hudson replicates the area of pink sky at the meeting of earth and air, just as Fleischbein did. He also borrows Mme Fleischbein's pose, with the bent left arm and straight right arm. The background of his subsequent *Creole Boy with a Moth* (fig. 55) repeats the format, and adds the vignette of a road receding into the background, again emulating Fleischbein's portrait of his wife.

Hudson, however, seems to have realized that modeling himself on Fleischbein might not take him far enough in New Orleans's competitive art world, where only several blocks from hisown studio, the powerhouse trio of Vaudechamp, Amans, and Lansot were sharing studio space on Royal Street. And he seems to have been smart enough to visually compare his works with theirs to figure out that they could

Figure 23
PORTRAIT OF A YOUNG GIRL WITH A ROSE
by Julien Hudson
1834, oil on canvas
courtesy of the Zigler Museum

Figure 24
DEATH OF BRITTANICUS
by Alexandre-Denis Abel de Pujol
n.d., pen and black ink, brown wash, with white gouache over graphite and red chalk
courtesy of the Metropolitan Museum of Art, gift of Mr. and Mrs. Bruno de Bayser, 2004.318
© The Metropolitan Museum of Art/Art Resource

Figure 25
THE APOTHEOSIS OF SAINT ROCH, STUDY FOR THE CEILING OF
THE CHAPEL OF SAINT ROCH IN THE CHURCH OF SAINT-SULPICE, PARIS
by Alexandre-Denis Abel de Pujol
ca. 1815–30, oil on canvas
courtesy of Réunion des Musées Nationaux/Art Resource, NY, P.46.1.163

do things he could not. Perhaps what clients wanted were not only skills, but the pedigree these colleagues shared: a French accent, as it were.

The gap between Hudson's first three signed works and the final works of his career suggests that in the interim Hudson went once more to Paris. It is not difficult to imagine that the New Orleans art world, now awash with Paris-trained competitors/colleagues, prompted Hudson to drink at the source, rather than at a stream. Thus, sometime between 1835 and 1837, when ship records place him back in the United States, Hudson was again in Paris, there most likely to work with French painter Alexandre-Denis Abel de Pujol.

Abel de Pujol had begun his training in his native Valenciennes before moving to Paris to study with David and thence entering the mainstream of official French art. He thrived within it, winning the Prix de Rome in 1811. The fruits of his immersion in classical culture can be seen in such critically approved subjects as the death of the Roman general Brittanicus, which was exhibited in Paris at the Salon of 1814 and whose surviving compositional drawing (fig. 24) reveals Abel de Pujol's style. By the time Hudson studied with him, Abel de Pujol had hit his stride as a painter of elaborate allegorical ceiling paintings and large-scale religious scenes (figs. 25 and 26). Nevertheless, his first critical success rested upon portraiture, of which he was a master. His own *Self-Portrait* (fig. 27) reveals a brooding, exciting directness, appropriate for the image of an ambitious young artist. And his monumental double portrait of Nicholas Legrand and his grandson Joseph-Adolphe (fig. 28) shows exactly what

Figure 26
ALLEGORICAL FIGURE OF THE
CITY OF PIACENZA, FOR A PENDENTIVE
IN THE CHAPEL OF ST. ROCH,
SAINT-SULPICE, PARIS
by Alexandre-Denis Abel de Pujol
1821, graphite, heightened with white, on beige paper
courtesy of the Metropolitan Museum of Art, purchase,
the David L. Klein Jr. Memorial Foundation, Inc. gift,
1984.66; © The Metropolitan Museum of Art / Art Resource

Figure 27
SELF-PORTRAIT
by Alexandre-Denis Abel de Pujol
1806, oil on canvas
courtesy of Réunion des Musées Nationaux/
Art Resource, NY

Hudson wanted to master. Both the artist and the sitters dominate their respective domains, uniting in a production that is a triumph of assured handling. The work is full of rich color, subdued, precise brushwork, and the sense of two distinct personalities: the grandfather confident and composed; the child inquisitive and open.[28] It is the direct antecedent of the sort of masterful double portrait by Vaudechamp (figs. 29 and 30), for example, that Hudson may have seen in 1830s New Orleans.

By the late 1830s, for an artist desiring to forge a link with the glories of the French past, Abel de Pujol was a logical choice. In fact, with Girodet's death in 1824, Antoine Gros's passing in 1835, and the geographical remove of Jean-Auguste-Dominique Ingres (1780–1867) from Paris to Italy, there were very few stars of the Davidian school left as teachers. While Abel de Pujol was not exactly in the same rank as his former classmates, he nonetheless was a successful artist. It is highly probable that one of Hudson's European contemporaries would have recommended Abel de Pujol to him—and equally probable that the recommendation came about because of those artists' own ties to what was in effect a Davidian mafia that tended to breed and encourage legacies over generations.[29]

Documentation of Hudson's presence in Abel de Pujol's studio cannot be found in official records. He is not listed in the inscriptions register of the École nationale supérieure des beaux-arts for 1824–31 or 1834–40, nor on any of the study cards that Abel de Pujol submitted to the Louvre to obtain permission for his students to work in the museum's galleries.[30] Yet that lack of documentation does not rule out Hudson as a student. Inscription information about Abel de

Figure 28
NICHOLAS LEGRAND AND HIS GRANDSON, JOSEPH-ADOLPHE DE PUJOL
by Alexandre-Denis Abel de Pujol
1815, oil on canvas
courtesy of the High Museum, purchased with funds from the Phoenix Society and purchased with funds given
by Alfred Austell Thornton in memory of Leila Austell Thornton and Albert Edward Thornton Sr.,
and Sarah Miller Venable and William Hoyt Venable, 1990.2

Figure 29
MADAME CLARA DUREL FORSTALL AND EUGÈNE FORSTALL
by Jean-Joseph Vaudechamp
1836, oil on canvas
The Historic New Orleans Collection, gift of Olga and Yvonne Tremoulet, 2005.0345.1

Figure 30
EDMOND JEAN FORSTALL AND DESIRÉE FORSTALL
by Jean-Joseph Vaudechamp
1836, oil on canvas
The Historic New Orleans Collection, gift of Olga and Yvonne Tremoulet, 2005.0345.3

Pujol's students varies from source to source.[31] In addition, thorough documentation of foreign students studying at the École nationale supérieure des beaux-arts did not begin until 1878.[32] And, just as in his previous trip, Hudson left no other trace in the public record.

Hudson returned to New Orleans on August 16, 1837, arriving on the *Scotland*.[33] His return was likely prompted by family tragedy rather than the termination of a course of study with Abel de Pujol. His sister Charlotte had died on February 28 of that year.[34] As his mother's eldest child, Hudson may have wanted to be there to console her. And given the fact that his other sister, Françoise, died within several months of his return, on November 21, it is safe to wonder if knowledge of a serious illness may have prompted his return.[35]

Although Hudson is listed in the 1838 New Orleans city directory as a painter residing at 120 Bienville Street, no more paintings dated prior to 1839 exist. These two 1839 portraits are the last surviving documented works of Hudson's career. They show both the possibilities and limits of the Parisian experience.

The late-career portrait of Jean Michel Fortier (fig. 31), shows Hudson reaching, with mixed results. In this, his largest work, the artist captures a vivid sense of personality and forthrightness in his sitter. He experiments with greater detail in this work than in previous compositions, witnessed by the sheet music Fortier holds, its notations clearly visible. Yet despite the newfound ambition evident in the Fortier portrait, Hudson comes close to skewing the composition's effect with Fortier's paw-like hand, which is out of proportion to its setting. Some of the infelicities of the portrait may be the inevitable result of the circumstances of the commission. The portrait was posthumous, ordered by Fortier's family. Thus, without a living model in front of him—perhaps even working from a yet-undiscovered source such as an older miniature—Hudson did not have the corrective balance of the sitter's presence. The apparent visual problems in the final work also remind the viewer of Hudson's inheritance from his New Orleans instructors; achieving proportion remained a challenge. And though Hudson continued his formal training, the Fortier portrait suggests that his last Parisian sojourn may have come too late. By 1837 Hudson had perhaps already realized his full artistic potential.

But another portrait dated the same year as *Jean Michel Fortier* complicates such an easy assessment of the artist's successes and shortcomings. This small *Portrait of a Man, Called a Self-Portrait* (fig. 9) is the masterpiece of Hudson's oeuvre. Like the Fortier portrait, it is signed and dated 1839, although the order of the two portraits cannot be determined. The artist positions the sitter in a fictive-oval surround that mimics and references his training as a miniaturist. Against a marshy, misty background, with a low horizon line bisected by areas of pink that break through the clouds, a young man at bust length poses at three-quarter view, turned to his left and the viewer's right. His reddish-brown hair is neatly combed, his face clean shaven, except for two dramatically wide sideburns that stretch to his chin. His patterned waistcoat, juxtaposed against an elegant black jacket, stock, and tie, draws the viewer's eye. Most striking are his distinctive facial features: widely spaced, oval, bluish eyes; a long, prominent, curving nose; and pursed cupid's-bow lips set above a slightly receding chin. If the atmospheric background, turn of the body, and oblique glance all

Figure 31
JEAN MICHEL FORTIER
by Julien Hudson
1839, oil on canvas
courtesy of the Collections of Louisiana State Museum, gift of Marguerite Fortier, 11321

carry over from Hudson's *Portrait of a Young Girl with a Rose* and *Creole Boy with a Moth*—and thus descend from Fleischbein—the entire composition is knitted together triumphantly with a new maturity. For the first time, Hudson smoothly synthesizes figure and landscape, making the figure seem to inhabit his space rather than seem drawn against it. Hudson's modeling also is more assured. He still begins as a draftsman, witnessed by the outlines of his subject's nose and eye sockets, as well as the edges of his clothing. Yet unlike in his other works, here delineation unites with plasticity. Lines help create borders, but also now add clarification, instead of separating forms into flattened patterns as in his other works. It is hard not to read the combination of assurance and charm in this portrait as coming from an artist reaching maturity after having undertaken further study.

No signed works by Hudson are known to postdate *Fortier* and *Portrait of a Man*. A small, unsigned and undated portrait, titled *Portrait of a Creole Gentleman* (fig. 10), surfaced at a New Orleans auction house in the early twenty-first century before being purchased by a private collector for the Dallas Museum of Art.[36] Based on its size and the sitter's distinctive resemblance to the sitter for *Portrait of a Man*, it was attributed at the time of its sale to Hudson. Its relatively modest size is consistent with the dimensions of the majority of the other secure works by Hudson. Its neutral background could suggest that it was completed after Hudson's training in France, where such a treatment was standard. Certainly, Hudson adopted that type of composition in the signed and dated Fortier portrait, which is indebted to a French example. Yet the Dallas picture's handling and modeling seem more assured than the rest of Hudson's signed works, with the exception of *Portrait of a Man*. The Dallas picture is certainly more successfully executed than the Fortier portrait, which would otherwise be its closest analogue in Hudson's oeuvre. Hudson may have been more comfortable working on a familiar, smaller scale, which might account for the work's seeming greater sophistication than the Fortier portrait.

The remaining evidence of Hudson's life is brief and can be quickly recounted. In 1840 he took on his only known pupil, George David Coulon (1822–1904). Then, in 1844, Hudson died, which we learn from Coulon and which is documented in the historical archive, though that selfsame documentation raises questions about the circumstances of his death. After 1844 the historic Hudson passed out of existence. His story, however, does not end there.

Despite the increasing societal and legal pressures brought to bear on them in the years leading up to the Civil War, Louisiana's free people of color continued to act as patrons and artists.[37] Portraits from the middle decades of the nineteenth century testify to the continuing function of free people of color as consumers, even if the identities of their portraitists remain undocumented. The successful career of French-born immigrant Jules Lion (figs. 32–36), a photographer, lithographer, and occasional portraitist, testifies to the possibilities that Hudson sought without success.

Historians have demonstrated the political, cultural, and economic decline of Louisiana's free people of color in the wake of the Civil War. Emancipation not only eliminated the legal distinction between those people of color who had been free before the war and those who had

Figure 32
VILLERE
by Jules Lion
1837, lithograph
The Historic New Orleans Collection, 1970.11.41

Figure 33
MARIUS S. BRINGIER
by Jules Lion
between 1837 and 1847, lithograph
The Historic New Orleans Collection, 1959.13.2

Figure 34
ANDRÉ MARTIN
by Jules Lion
1841, lithograph
The Historic New Orleans Collection, 1959.13.75

Figure 35
ACHILLE LION
by Jules Lion
between 1837 and 1847, lithograph
The Historic New Orleans Collection, 1970.11.22

Figure 36
ELIZA FIELD, ELIZA DUBOURG FIELD, AND ODILE FIELD
by Jules Lion
1838, lithograph
The Historic New Orleans Collection, 1970.11.141

Figure 37
THE PRICE OF BLOOD
by Thomas Satterwhite Noble
1868, oil on canvas
courtesy of the Morris Museum of Art, Augusta, Georgia, 1989.03.237

Figure 38
THE QUADROON
by George Fuller
1880, oil on canvas
courtesy of the Metropolitan Museum of Art, gift of George A. Hearn, 10.64.3
© The Metropolitan Museum of Art / Art Resource

Figure 39
CREOLE WOMAN ACCOMPANIED BY CONFEDERATE SYMBOLS
attributed to Arthur Lumley
ca. 1861, watercolor
courtesy of a private collection

been enslaved, but actively eroded privileges that members of the former caste had once enjoyed.[38] With emancipation and Reconstruction, Hudson's world as it had existed for a century vanished. In its place were whites and blacks—and works by white artists that depicted people of color not as individuals with agency in their representations, but as Others and objects of pity, whether an imagined antebellum image of a planter selling his own son (fig. 37), or a young woman working as a field slave or sharecropper (fig. 38), or, in one dramatic case, as a politicized allegorical representation of the Confederacy itself (fig. 39).

AN ARTIST'S LEGACY

In 1901 the aged painter George Coulon compiled his artistic autobiography and an anecdotal history of artists in New Orleans.[39] In this never-published manuscript Coulon mentioned his former teacher exactly twice. First, when describing his own formation, he inserted Hudson into a lineage of mentors: "In the later part of [18]40 I took lessons in portrait painting with *Julien Hudson*. Born in this city, he was a pupil of Abel de Pujol of Paris."[40] After listing other artists under whom he studied, including Leon D. Pomarede (1807 or 1811–1892), Toussaint François Bigot (1794–1869), François Fleischbein, and Antonio Mondelli (born ca. 1799), Coulon sums up Hudson's career in one sentence: "Julien Hudson, (portrait painter) native of New O, he studied in Paris in 1837 died in 1844."[41] From Coulon—the only contemporary commentator on Hudson and the only one who knew him personally—we learn that Hudson was born in New Orleans, studied in Paris, and died. There is no mention of Hudson's race. This suggests multiple possibilities, none of which may be definitively tested and proven. When working with his pupil sixty years before, was Hudson passing as white? Or was Coulon—who both represented the next generation during Hudson's career and functioned retrospectively in 1901 as its historian—aware, but indifferent? In that case, perhaps for Coulon, Hudson's status as a Louisiana-born artist and his expatriate instruction in the Davidian school were the details of his life worthy of remembrance, not his putative skin color or racial ancestry.

Coulon penned his history for the benefit of another artist, Bror Anders Wikstrom (1854–1909).[42] He wrote as one artist to another, as a peer to another peer, about a mentor. Thus it is understandable that what mattered was not Hudson's race, but the role he played both in New Orleans's and Coulon's artistic histories. The Hudson of the Coulon manuscript is thus either a teacher and artist whose skill transcends racial limitations/categorization, or a man who had to hide his identity. The absence of any language indicating his race opens fascinating interpretive possibilities to the contemporary reader.

Figure 40
BOY WITH A ROSE
by George David Coulon
ca. 1842, oil on canvas
courtesy of the Collections of Louisiana State Museum, 04931

The tangible legacy of Hudson as a teacher is apparent in one of Coulon's early paintings, *Boy with a Rose*. The positioning of the grave child close to the surface of the picture plane evokes Hudson's treatment of his youthful sitters in *Creole Boy with a Moth* and *Portrait of a Young Girl with a Rose*, as does the flower prop held in his right hand. Like Hudson, the young Coulon had not quite mastered successful three-dimensional modeling of his figure's form, even though he knew where shadows should fall.

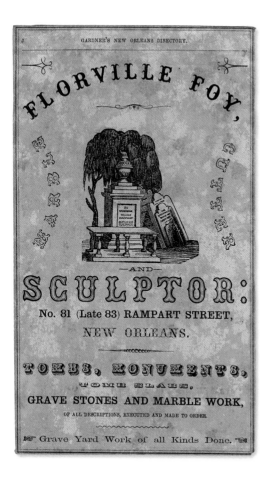

Figure 41
ADVERTISEMENT FOR
FLORVILLE FOY
from *Gardner's New Orleans Directory*
The Historic New Orleans Collection, 1974.25.1.17

The realm of interpretive possibility was not to persist in other textual treatments of Hudson. While Coulon penned his race-less description of Hudson, other writers began assigning him a distinct racial identity. Coulon wrote his memoir at roughly the same time that new histories of Louisiana art and culture began making their way to bookshop and library shelves. In these published works, Hudson lost the open-ended identity he possessed in Coulon's text and took on a distinct racial identity: that of a "colored" artist.

The year before Coulon finished his memoir, Henry Rightor published an edited volume titled *Standard History of New Orleans*. In the chapter on literature and art, contributor Mrs. A. G. Durno included Hudson in the single paragraph she devoted to nineteenth-century New Orleans artists, describing him as "a very light colored man who painted portraits which were much esteemed."[43] As Patricia Brady has pointed out, Durno was the first published commentator to ascribe a racial identity to Hudson, though it should be noted that this reference came from an individual who was not herself involved in the art world.[44]

In his 1911 *Nos hommes et notre histoire* (*Our People and Our History*) Rodolphe Desdunes shared the discouraging story of Alexandre Pickhil, a New Orleans painter of color who knew a sad life of opposition and destroyed his masterpiece rather than face criticism.[45] The tragic tale of an artist thwarted by a hostile world was picked up by compilers both of Louisiana and African American art.[46]

Yet as Brady has discussed in her essay, the historic Alexandre Pickhil did not exist, which accounts for his lack of surviving works and his absence from New Orleans archival records. Instead, the invented name embroidered from one of Hudson's nicknames seems to embody what Desdunes and the community of free people of color remembered about the historic Julien Hudson over fifty years later. An artist with some version of the name "Pickhil" lived in New Orleans. He was unhappy; he knew adversity in his work; he destroyed his art; and he died under a cloud. Desdunes never mentioned "Julien Hudson" in his account; nevertheless, other compilers after Desdunes who were already aware of Hudson added the writer's quasi-fictitious Pickhil to their lists, creating in effect two distinct artists of color in the history of New Orleans art—although only Hudson had any signed works to his name.

Within a generation of Durno and Desdunes, John Smith Kendall in his 1922 *History of New Orleans* described Hudson as "an octoroon, whose portraits were, in his day, considered good."[47] Kendall's description of Hudson echoes Durno's earlier phrasing so closely that one might assume he used it as a source for his own work.

Hudson is absent from one of the earliest post-Coulon surveys of Louisiana art. Published the same year as Kendall's *History of New Orleans*, Dr. Isaac Monroe Cline's "Art and Artists in New Orleans Since Colonial Times" makes no mention of the young artist.[48] Cline, a physician and meteorologist by profession, accumulated one of the largest and earliest collections of Louisiana art. His omission of Hudson is particularly confusing, since in 1920 he donated or sold (the exact nature of the transaction is unclear) Julien Hudson's *Portrait of a Man* to the Louisiana State Museum.[49] Perhaps Cline omitted Hudson from his narrative because he did not consider him a "distinguished" artist, as he termed Jacques Amans, Jean-Joseph Vaudechamp, François Fleischbein, and other native and foreign-born practitioners mentioned in his article.[50] But because he likewise omitted Jules Lion, Florville Foy, and both Warburg brothers, one must wonder whether Cline's exclusion of Hudson was part of a blanket elimination of any artist of color.[51]

Hudson did show up in the other early-twentieth-century survey of Louisiana art, Ben Earl Looney's 1935 "Historical Sketch of Art in Louisiana." After running through the fine arts, Looney appears to have tacked Hudson on after his discussion of architecture. When discussing architect Jacques Nicolas Bussière de Pouilly, Looney mentions that "It is interesting to note in passing that many of the tombs designed by de Pouilly were executed by Floraville [sic] Foy [figs. 41 and 42], a light colored man, who was a graduate of one of the French training schools and skilled in the carving of marble. Another negro artist of the past in Louisiana was Julian [sic] Hudson who painted portraits of distinction."[52] Not only was Hudson tacked on as an afterthought—with no reference to his status as a free person; he was also, by this time, not mixed, but full-on black, "a negro."

By the 1930s, art historical treatments of Hudson invariably mentioned his race. And in 1938, for as-yet-undiscovered reasons, one of his surviving works, an 1839 portrait, became forever linked to the artist's own likeness—a circumstance that would enshrine Hudson posthumously in histories of African American art. When the portrait entered the collection of the Louisiana State Museum in 1920, it was listed simply as *Portrait of a Man* (fig. 9).[53] It was subsequently cataloged as such in the 1934 museum handbook.[54] Yet in 1938, when the painting was featured as part of a series of

Figure 42
CHILD WITH DRUM
by Florville Foy
ca. 1838, marble
courtesy of the Collections of Louisiana State Museum, gift of M. Marcell, 00216

loan exhibitions celebrating historic Louisiana art at the Delgado (now New Orleans) Museum of Art, Ethel Hutson, Delgado's secretary to the board of trustees and supervisor of the WPA Art Project, claimed in a local newspaper review article that the work was a self-portrait. She wrote,

> *Jules Hudson, an octoroon, and a "free man of color," was another native New Orleans artist of this period. His self-portrait shows pronounced Jewish as well as Negroid characters. He was a pupil of Abel de Pujol in Paris, and on his return to New Orleans in 1821, taught art as well as painting portraits and miniatures, George D. Coulon being one of his pupils!* [55]

Hutson's claim seemed authoritative. Yet upon closer inspection of both the text and the image it purports to describe, questions arise. How could Hutson have been so secure in her claims? As Patricia Brady noted more than fifty years later, "The portrait . . . could be a fair man of color; he could equally be French, Spanish, Latin American."[56] Hutson provided no factual evidence for her identification of the painting's sitter.[57] Furthermore, she claimed to have spotted not just African but Jewish blood in her reading of the State Museum portrait. This is certainly odd if the painting is to be taken as a self-portrait, as there is no evidence of any Semitic ancestry in Hudson's family. It is likely that she based her analysis on the sitter's distinct physiognomy, and then covered her treatment with period stereotyping, grounded in the notion that Jews have long, exaggerated noses.

Once Hutson identified the work as a self-portrait, however, the label stuck. Indeed, the idea—however erroneously reached—that Julien Hudson had painted himself flourished. In the wake of the Harlem Renaissance—the early-twentieth-century cultural movement created and sustained by African American writers, intellectuals, and artists—a growing desire to document and promote African Americans' historic cultural contributions led to a steady stream of scholarship. And Hudson, as an early exemplar, with a self-portrait in tow, fit right in. References to the "self-portrait" appeared in seminal African American histories of art and culture, ranging from influential art historical monographs such as James A. Porter's 1943 *Modern Negro Art* to popular histories such as Arna Bontemps's 1948 *Story of the Negro*, among others.[58] Hudson's self-portrait was perhaps most dramatically described in Cedric Dover's 1960 *American Negro Art* as being "made more remarkable by an ample nose which qualifies him, in this respect, as a lesser Cyrano de Bergerac among Negroes."[59]

Following the Civil Rights Movement of the 1950s and '60s, Hudson's self-portrait received further attention during a second wave of African American art scholarship.[60] But perhaps most significantly, at least in terms of exposure, the painting and its maker reached their widest audience of viewers and scholars through its inclusion in ground-breaking exhibitions of self-portraiture and African American art such as *Ten Afro-American Artists of the Nineteenth Century* (1967, Howard University Art Gallery); *Reflections in Black* (1970, La Jolla Museum of Art); *American Self-Portraits, 1670–1973* (1974, National Portrait Gallery, Smithsonian Institution, and the Indianapolis Museum of Art); *Two Centuries of Black American Art* (1976, Los Angeles County Museum of Art);

and *Selections of Nineteenth-Century Afro-American Art* (1976, Metropolitan Museum of Art).[61] By the time of its presentation at the Metropolitan Museum of Art, the work, according to curator Regenia A. Perry, had achieved the status of "the earliest known portrait of an Afro-American artist," while Hudson himself became "the earliest documented professional Afro-American painter in the South."[62]

More recent commentators have continued to use the supposed self-portrait as a key to understanding the elusive historical figure of Hudson. In her influential survey text of African American art, Samella Lewis uses Hudson as a way into understanding the world of his class:

> *The facial features of the figure indicate that the artist was of mixed ancestry, and the manner of dress suggests that he enjoyed the privileges of gentry. As a free mulatto in New Orleans, Hudson was exposed to the French tradition and to a lifestyle that reflected a level of elegance and flamboyance not then found elsewhere in the United States. His self-portrait helps depict the flavor and quality of life that was available to many freemen in nineteenth-century New Orleans.[63]*

When including the painting in the 2006 exhibition *Portraits of a People* (Addison Gallery of American Art), curator Gwendolyn DuBois Shaw highlighted the ambiguity of the sitter's features, suggesting that the painting offered "no overt physiognomic characteristics that may be read as stereotypically African." Instead, she read the sitter's features as a possible index of the historically intermediate position between black and white that the artist would have occupied:

> *[T]he artist may have chosen to underscore his white heritage in the almost grotesque over-pronouncement of an exceedingly narrow nose and reduction of the lips to a full yet childish pout. In these exaggerated features there is perhaps an unconscious indication of the artist's own anxiety over the physical markers in his face of an ambiguous racial designation.[64]*

These examples reflect broader trends in portraiture scholarship that view the portrait-making enterprise as being a collaborative construction of identity mediated among the triangular relationship of sitter, artist, and viewer.[65]

The perpetuation of the unproven idea that the Louisiana State Museum's painting is a self-portrait is not due to lack of evidence otherwise. Three times in recent decades, scholars have followed the paper trail and pointed out the gap in documentation.[66] Yet the identification persists. In some cases, particularly in reference works, compilers routinely repeat previously published information, without re-verifying the accuracy of the sources.[67] And, in fairness, they have no reason to mistrust individual information, being more concerned about documentation of artists, rather than the accuracy of the identities of the sitter. The fact that the question has been raised

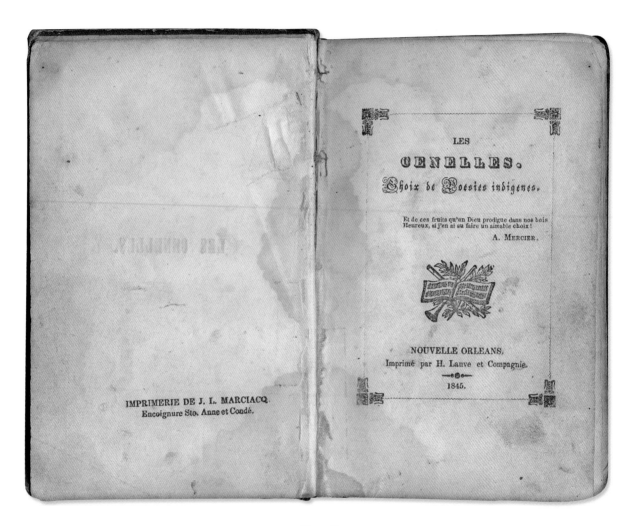

Figure 43
LES CENELLES: CHOIX DE POÉSIES INDIGÈNES
by Armand Lanusse, editor and contributor
New Orleans: H. Lauve, 1845
The Historic New Orleans Collection, 87-632-RL

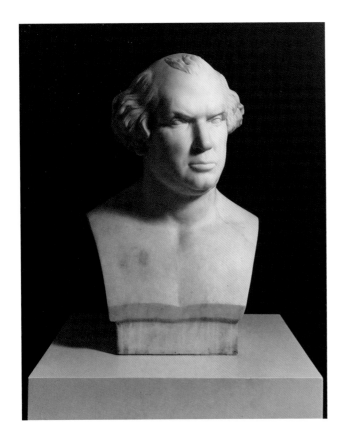 

Figure 44
JOHN YOUNG MASON
by Eugène Warburg
1855, marble
courtesy of the Virginia Historical Society, 1927.21

Figure 45
FOREVER FREE
by Edmonia Lewis
1867, marble
courtesy of Howard University Gallery of Art, Washington DC

by historians, rather than art historians or curators, in Louisiana publications dealing with history, rather than specialized art historical journals, must also help explain why the Louisiana State Museum portrait has not been more closely scrutinized. Simply put, the most sustained critical scholarship on the portrait has been carried out by scholars in another discipline, whose findings have often been relegated to regional—as opposed to mainstream—publications. When the portrait has been featured in literature devoted to art history, writers either have not done their due diligence in canvassing scholarship beyond their own discipline, or have not searched for evidence of the sitter's identity. Thus, the unsubstantiated identification has been repeated and built upon, in an endless loop.

It must also be acknowledged that questioning the identification threatens to disappoint viewers by invalidating the painting's status as one of the oldest surviving images of a *sitter* of African descent by a *painter* of African descent. In that sense, skepticism, no matter how firmly grounded in caution, takes away the one tangible success that has been attached to Hudson's brief career—his recording of his own features. It also might inadvertently be considered a case of revisionism that undoes one of the best-known icons of African American art, even though the painting is unassailably by Hudson.

Louisiana itself poses complications for scholars of African American art.[68] Despite Hudson's inclusion in twentieth-century identity politics–oriented surveys of African American art, it is, as Shaw noted, hard to locate racial difference in his works—or, for that matter, in those of his mixed-race contemporaries. This is due to the fact that, as free people of color in New Orleans, they lived in a white-normative world. For young, privileged free men of color, the European world was the model of education, and artistic traditions were modeled on European examples. The verse-poetry of *Les Cenelles* (1845) (fig. 43), an anthology penned by free men of color, adopted the formal language and style of French poetry.[69] In the visual and plastic arts, New Orleans sculptor Eugène Warburg immersed himself in Rome, the epicenter of classicism in the eighteenth and nineteenth centuries. Warburg's single surviving work, the bust of John Young Mason (fig. 44), firmly allies itself with the antique through its reference to Roman portrait busts.[70] But since Warburg died in 1859, he did not live long enough to adapt the antique vocabulary of classicism to a contemporary subject dealing with race, unlike his former colleague in Rome, the half African American, half Chippewa sculptor Edmonia Lewis (ca. 1845–ca. 1911), whose *Forever Free* (fig. 45) depicts the breaking of the chains of slavery.[71]

The portrayal of enslaved people of color in genre paintings before the Civil War is virtually unknown in Louisiana. In the North, one of the earliest genre paintings is German-born, Philadelphia-based John Lewis Krimmel's 1813 *The Quilting Frolic* (fig. 46), a party scene that includes an exaggeratedly caricatured pair of capering black servants. In contrast, the best-known such work in Louisiana art is the much-later 1860 *A Plantation Burial* (fig. 47) by John Antrobus (1831–1907), an English-born artist who had previously worked in the North.[72] Although this moody, evocative scene definitely treats the slaves as Others, through the device of the artist as

Figure 46
THE QUILTING FROLIC
by John Lewis Krimmel
1813, oil on canvas
courtesy of Winterthur Museum and Country Estate, 1953.0178.002

Figure 47
A PLANTATION BURIAL
by John Antrobus
1860, oil on canvas
The Historic New Orleans Collection, 1960.46

Figure 48
CLARA DE LA MOTTE
by José Francisco Xavier de Salazar y Mendoza
ca. 1795, oil on canvas
The Historic New Orleans Collection, 1981.213

visual eavesdropper (at left) who acts as a surrogate for the viewer, it does not fall into the habit of stereotyping them by markers of difference, as Krimmel does with his pop-eyed, grinning figures.[73]

It is in portraits that Louisiana's people of color—and free people of color in particular—make their appearance. We return to the early portrait of Marianne Celeste Dragon (fig. 1) from the circle of Salazar y Mendoza. Wearing a sumptuous blue satin *robe à la française* and seated at an elegant marble-topped *guéridon*, Dragon idly arranges a basket of flowers, some of which she has transferred to her bodice. The device is likely an already dated iconographical trope equating her youth and beauty with nature. She wears her hair according to the French style *à la hérisson* (or in the "hedgehog" style), adorned with a fillet of pearls, matched by a strand around her throat.[74]

First and foremost, Dragon's portrait constructs her as a fashionable young woman. Her family most likely commissioned the work to signal her availability. In 1799, around the time this painting is believed to have been made, she married André Dimitry, who, like her father, was of Greek origin.[75] The only visual markers that one could interpret as indices of mixed racial ancestry are the texture of her hair, as well as what seems to be an olive skin tone. Both seem distinctly different from the way Salazar himself represented the hair and flesh of Clara de la Motte (fig. 48), for example.

Dragon and her family's interests in deemphasizing any markers of racial Otherness were mirrored by her subsequent life. After her marriage, she passed as white, a strategy that succeeded until her grandson George Pandelly was elected to the Board of Assistant Aldermen in 1853, at which point Victor Wiltz (Pandelly's political opponent) challenged Pandelly's appointment by accusing him of having women of mixed race as his maternal grandmother and great-grandmother.[76]

But even if Dragon herself eventually entered the white community, later surviving portraits of New Orleans sitters of color—sitters who were likely unable to pass—also follow dominant conventions of representation that matter-of-factly represent appearance, rather than Otherness (figs. 49–51). This is true in portraits that seem to have been commissioned works, such as examples by the French immigrants Aimable-Désiré Lansot (fig. 52) and Charles Colson (1810–?) (fig. 53). And it is also apparently the case in a portrait by François Fleischbein of his servant Betsy (fig. 21)—a painting probably spurred by the artist's own interest in and gratitude to a member of his household. Fleischbein seems to have been more fascinated by Betsy's expression than her skin tone. Indeed, her sideways gaze and partially turned head recur in depictions of many of the artist's sitters. This matter-of-factness and lack of emphasis on flesh pigmentation, for example, seems distinctly different from a northeastern portrait of a servant of color by Gilbert Stuart (1755–1828). Stuart's portrayal of Hercules (fig. 54), George Washington's family cook, focuses the viewer's attention on the sitter's African features through its concentration on the glazes and variegated pigments that make up Hercules' face. And while some of this relates to Stuart's technique—he always began with his sitters' faces and then worked his way outward—the end result is that physiognomy and skin tones are the focal point of the portrait.[77]

Figure 49
PORTRAIT OF A FREE WOMAN OF COLOR
by Louis-Antoine Collas
1829, oil on canvas
courtesy of the New Orleans Museum of Art, gift of Dr. I. M. Cline, 38.1

Figure 50
PORTRAIT OF A LADY, PRESUMED TO BE A FREE WOMAN OF COLOR
by an unknown artist
1857, pastel, gouache, and oil on paper
courtesy of Leah M. Coleman

Figure 51
PORTRAIT OF A CREOLE GIRL
by Mariette Darney
1846, watercolor and pencil on paper
courtesy of Elle Shushan

Figure 52
PORTRAIT OF A CREOLE WOMAN OF COLOR
by Aimable-Désiré Lansot
ca. 1845, oil on canvas
courtesy of the Collections of Louisiana State Museum, 1993.105

Figure 53
CREOLE WOMAN
by Charles-Jean-Baptiste Colson
ca. 1837, oil on canvas
courtesy of the Collections of Louisiana State Museum, 05792

Figure 54
PORTRAIT OF GEORGE WASHINGTON'S COOK
by Gilbert Stuart
ca. 1795–97, oil on canvas
© *Museo Thyssen-Bornemisza, Madrid*

Figure 55
CREOLE BOY WITH A MOTH
by Julien Hudson
1835, oil on canvas
courtesy of a private collection; photo courtesy of Fodera Fine Art Conservation, Ltd.

Figure 56
PORTRAIT OF A BLACK MAN
by Julien Hudson
1835, oil on canvas
pre-conservation photo courtesy of Didier Inc.

Figure 57
WILLIAM CLAIBORNE II
by Jean-Joseph Vaudechamp
1831, oil on canvas
*The Historic New Orleans Collection, bequest of
Clarisse Claiborne Grima, 1981.376.1*

Even when Hudson depicts sitters who seem to be of color, as in *Creole Boy with a Moth* (fig. 55) and *Portrait of a Black Man* (also called *Portrait of a Man in a Turban* and *Gentleman in a Turban*, fig. 56), their skin tones are the only markers that differentiate the portraits from those of his other, supposedly white sitters—or from the ways his Louisiana and European colleagues represent sitters, whether white or of color (fig. 57). Is this because, having lived in a white-normative society, as a member of a group that self-identified with other free people, regardless of color, Hudson and his colleagues did not identify with blackness? Or did their Francophone identity have stronger pull? Recent research into the manumission of slaves owned by free people of color in New Orleans has brought forward evidence that owners freed slaves with Gallic ancestry more frequently than those who were strictly African or Anglo-African.[78] This tendency suggests that at least some members of the community of free people of color, Hudson's milieu, prized their French cultural heritage over any similarities in skin tone that may have existed between them and their enslaved counterparts. Rodolphe Desdunes himself began his history with free men of color who served under Andrew Jackson during the War of 1812. Like Athena springing fully formed from the head of Zeus, his heroes step into his history as free individuals, already part of a seamless community, without any discussion of African or enslaved antecedents.[79]

Twenty-first-century viewers who wish to possess a racially visible Julien Hudson, not to mention a self-portrait by an artist of color, may find questions about the sitter's identity unsettling, or even disappointing. And efforts to untangle the myth created by Ethel Hutson and perpetuated by art historians and museum curators alike may be interpreted as an attempt to erase the issue of race from Hudson's work. But tantalizing—and potentially more satisfying—questions involving race and patronage still surround two of his other works, *Creole Boy with a Moth* and *Portrait of a Black Man*, both signed and dated 1835.

Creole Boy with a Moth shows a little boy standing in a landscape, turned at a three-quarter angle to his right. He wears a white shirt and trousers with a black jacket and large, floppy white tie. In his right hand, he holds a moth. The positioning of the figure in the landscape, with the horizon line below the level of the sitter's shoulders, is highly reminiscent of Fleischbein's portrait of his wife (fig. 18) as well as numerous examples produced by other European itinerants. The landscape reveals a curving river that runs parallel to the road. The boy has short curly hair, dark eyes, and a rosy complexion that suggests mixed blood.

Portrait of a Black Man depicts its sitter in an interior, seated against a dark background, at bust length. Slightly turned to his right as well, he wears a black suit and tie with a vivid scarlet turban wrapped in a gold, red-bordered cloth. His skin tone is much darker than the little boy's. He also sports a trim beard, whose white hairs suggest middle age, although his commanding presence reveals a self-assured man in the prime of his life.

As previously noted, portraits of sitters of color are not infrequent in antebellum Louisiana art. But they are for the most part by white artists. Hudson's signature on these works places them among a rare group of portraits of people of color made by a person of color. They join the scarce company of works such *Portrait of a Man* (fig. 58) by Joshua Johnson (ca. 1763–after 1824)—a mixed-race, free painter of color in early-nineteenth-century Baltimore who is, before Hudson, the earliest documented free painter of color in American history.[80]

If one assumes whiteness—or at least predominantly Caucasian blood—in the sitter of Hudson's *Portrait of a Young Girl with a Rose* from the previous year, these 1835 portraits indicate that he worked with both white and mixed-race clients. Such openness would have been natural in cosmopolitan New Orleans. Yet the easy assumption of whiteness on the part of the little girl is not as facile as a glance at the canvas suggests. Free people of color ran the gamut of skin tones. Indeed, nineteenth-century travel literature contains numerous examples of commentators startled by the difficulty in telling the difference between white and black in the exotic visual culture of New Orleans. As the British traveler George William Featherstonhaugh remarked in 1845, "A woman may be as fair as any European, and have no symptom of negro blood about her; she may have received a virtuous education, have been brought up with the greatest tenderness, may possess various accomplishments, and may be eminently calculated to act the part of a faithful wife and tender mother," but in actuality be a quadroon.[81] As the nineteenth century wore on, photography also provided evidence of the trickiness of visual signifiers of race, particularly through the diffusion of images of ex-slaves who, for all intents and purposes, looked just as white as their purported northern viewers (fig. 59).[82]

Figure 58
PORTRAIT OF A MAN
by Joshua Johnson
ca. 1805–10, oil on canvas
courtesy of Bowdoin College Museum of Art, Brunswick, Maine,
museum purchase, George Otis Hamlin Fund

Figure 59
REBECCA, A SLAVE GIRL FROM NEW ORLEANS
by Charles Paxson
1864, carte-de-visite
The Historic New Orleans Collection,
gift of Virginia T. Mosley, 1980.185

For that matter, the circumstances surrounding the commissioning of the portrait of Jean Michel Fortier also speak to the complexities of assuming easy binary oppositions between black and white in Hudson's patrons. The portrait has often erroneously been identified as that of Michel Fortier II, who commanded a battalion of free people of color during the Battle of New Orleans. It is instead an image of that man's son.[83] But if the Jean Michel Fortier depicted in Hudson's portrait did not have a military connection with communities of color, he certainly had a personal one. Although he never married, he maintained a long-term relationship with a free woman of color, with whom he fathered several children. These family members ostensibly commissioned this portrait after Fortier's death.[84] Was Hudson the go-to artist for free people of color wishing to have portraits made, in a spirit of keeping work in the community? Did the earlier portraits' patronage, as well as style, generate new commissions?

The portraits of the little boy and the gentleman in a turban lost their identities and provenances when they entered the art market: the former was sold at auction in New York in 2000 under a modified version of its title, with the moth identified as a butterfly; the latter belonged to a New Orleans dealer for years before its eventual sale to a private collection.[85] Like the subject in *Portrait of a Young Girl,* we have no firm information about the sitters' identities. We only know that whoever commissioned them had the means to do so.

Yet the historical archive may provide clues to the provenance of *Creole Boy with a Moth.* This painting's presence at Melrose Plantation in the early twentieth century brings Hudson's story into orbit with one of Louisiana's most famous—and mythologized—families of color, the Metoyers of Natchitoches. The linkage between *Creole Boy* and the Metoyer family allows for the possibility that a third portrait by a currently unidentified artist may be by Hudson.

The history of the storied Metoyer family began in 1765 with the extramarital relationship between Claude Thomas Pierre Metoyer, a French merchant posted at the military outpost of Natchitoches, Louisiana, and Marie Thérèse, an enslaved woman familiarly known as Coincoin whom he leased from her owner. Over the course of twenty years, the couple had ten children. Following her own manumission in 1778, Coincoin steadily bought her children, including those whose births predated her relationship with Metoyer, out of slavery, even while she settled and developed lands along the Cane River. Under the leadership of her eldest son, Augustin, the family built a plantation—originally known as Yucca—to cultivate indigo, tobacco, and cotton. The family greatly expanded its holdings, becoming one of the wealthiest families of color in Louisiana. Besides their business activities, the Metoyers also assumed leadership roles in their community, exemplified by Augustin Metoyer's funding of a church built to serve the parish, an act of philanthropy commemorated in a life-size portrait by the little-known artist J. B. Feuille. Financial reverses in the mid-nineteenth-century agricultural economy led to money problems, and the family lost the plantation in 1847.[86]

Descendants of the Metoyer family remained in the Cane River area, even while the plantation they built was acquired by two subsequent white families—most significantly, the Henry family in

1884. Called "Melrose" by this time, the house became the center of an early-twentieth-century bohemian community of white writers, artists, and craftspeople, encouraged and presided over by Carmelite "Cammie" G. Henry (1871–1948).[87]

Much of the mystique of Melrose—and the popularization of the Metoyer family story— sprang from the combined efforts of Lyle Saxon (1891–1946) and François Mignon (1899–1981). Saxon was a writer who spun extended stays at Melrose into written gold through articles and novels, such as *Children of Strangers* (1937).[88] The younger Mignon—born Frank VerNooy Mineah—was the virtual Man Who Came to Dinner, a self-christened art expert and historian who arrived at the plantation in the 1930s and stayed for decades, crafting a dramatic, yet exaggerated and predominantly baseless, history of the plantation and region through lectures and a regular column called the "Cane River Memo" in the *Natchitoches Enterprise*.[89]

Saxon and Mignon showed particular interest in depictions of free people of color. The men jointly owned the monumental pastel by Hudson's contemporary Jules Lion of Ashur Moses Nathan and Achille Lion (fig. 60), a double portrait, relatively rare in Louisiana art, and one that purportedly depicts a white father in an affectionate embrace with his mixed-race son.[90] It must be noted, however, that given the creativeness with which Saxon and Mignon approached history, their identification of the subjects should be treated with caution. In addition, the signature of this work differs radically from any other known Lion example.[91]

But regardless of Saxon and Mignon's creative histories, *Creole Boy with a Moth* seems to have been at Melrose Plantation some time prior to 1925. A photograph of the painting is pasted into an album compiled by Saxon and housed today in the Cammie G. Henry Research Center at Northwestern State University, in Natchitoches, Louisiana.[92] According to a handwritten date on the inside front cover, the album was begun in 1925. Midway through the album, on a page marked "Mulatto Portraits" (fig. 61), a black and white photo of what is recognizably *Creole Boy* appears next to a photograph of a painting thought to depict Marie Agnes Poissot Metoyer (fig. 64), which also is now housed at the Henry Research Center.[93] Underneath *Creole Boy* is the handwritten inscription "Domonic Metoyer/1836." The photo mounted in the album seems to be a cropped duplicate of a larger print showing the painting outside, leaning against a railing or side of a building, presumably at Melrose, with the same inscription in ink on the back.[94]

Despite the identification, the actual identity of the sitter for *Creole Boy* is unclear, due to the painting's uncertain provenance. There were several young male Metoyer children in the 1830s in several branches of the family (including more than one child whose first or middle name was Domonic), although the economic circumstances of their various parents helps narrow the list of potential candidates. Two of the likeliest are Nelcourt Baptiste Metoyer (1827–1850 or 1852) or his brother Auguste Paulin Metoyer (1829–1836), the two sons of Auguste Augustin Metoyer, son of Nicolas Augustin Metoyer. That branch of the family lived in New Orleans in the 1830s, where they easily could have come into contact with Hudson. In addition, Auguste Augustin Metoyer (fig. 62) and his wife Marie-Thérèse Carmelite "Melite" Anty (fig. 63) are generally considered by

Figure 60
ASHUR MOSES NATHAN AND SON (ACHILLE)
by Jules Lion
1845, pastel
portrait owned by Ann & Jack Brittain and children, photograph by Don Sepulvado

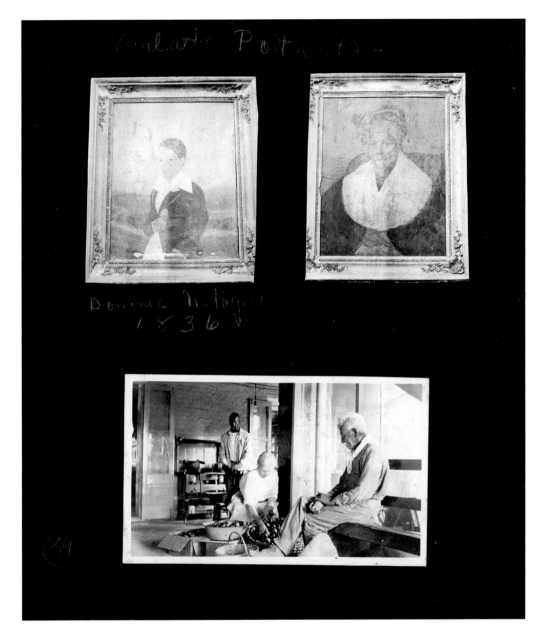

Figure 61
PAGE FROM SAXON ALBUM
by Lyle Saxon
ca. 1925, photoprints
courtesy of Cammie G. Henry Research Center, Watson Library,
Northwestern State University of Louisiana

Figure 62
AUGUSTE AUGUSTIN METOYER
by an unknown artist
ca. 1830s, oil on canvas
courtesy of Cammie G. Henry Research Center, Watson Library,
Northwestern State University of Louisiana

Figure 63
MARIE-THÉRÈSE METOYER
by an unknown artist
ca. 1830s, oil on canvas
courtesy of Cammie G. Henry Research Center, Watson Library,
Northwestern State University of Louisiana

scholars to be the subjects of two other portraits once at Melrose, now in the Henry Research Center, painted by a different and as yet unidentified artist.[95] The use of the moth—like the butterfly, a symbol of the soul—in the little boy's hand offers the tantalizing possibility that this is a memorial portrait. If so, the question of whether this is indeed a posthumous portrait of Auguste Paulin Metoyer arises. But given the known provenance of the other Metoyer family portraits that passed through Melrose, the sitter could also conceivably be Charles Achille Metoyer (b. 1830), son of Jean-Baptiste Augustin Metoyer.[96]

Although the exact identity of the little boy may not be recuperable, the matching dimensions and frames (visible in Saxon's album) of the signed, dated Hudson portrait *Creole Boy with a Moth* and the unsigned portrait reputedly of Marie Agnes Poissot Metoyer (fig. 64) suggest a natural relationship between the two, as does their presence together at Melrose—even though *Creole Boy* seems to have vanished from the plantation before the auction of its contents in 1970. How the portraits wound up at Melrose in the 1920s or 1930s is unclear, although the research center staff has acknowledged that evidence suggests members of the Henry circle wrangled them in various ways from Metoyer descendants who had inherited them. This wrangling ranged from bartering to "borrowing" and neglecting to return them.[97]

The portrait thought to depict Marie Agnes Poissot Metoyer suffered disfiguring cleaning and overpainting between the date of the scrapbook photo and 1947, when it was described by François Mignon as "a badly retouched portrait of Grandpère Augustin's wife. . . . It dates from about 1836."[98] Close study of the pre-treatment photograph mounted in Saxon's album reveals a markedly different work, one much more sophisticated and seemingly the work of a skilled portraitist (fig. 65). Could Hudson have been the artist? The painting's current condition renders the question unanswerable, yet the work does seem connected to *Creole Boy*. It is therefore not that far-fetched to wonder about the identity of the sitter in *Portrait of a Black Man*, signed and dated the same year, another painting without a provenance but with a signature. Was this sitter a Metoyer, as well? If so, a new angle on Hudson's life is suggested: a known painter of color patronized by one of the wealthiest families of color of his day. While patronage might have crossed color lines, it also might have reified them.

The suggestion of patronage based on race is one that the art world has been happy to supply in recent years. As southern art has itself become increasingly visible as a field, witnessed in the past several decades by an increasing number of museum exhibitions, and particularly by the creation of museums with a southern focus, Hudson has become a convenient name upon which to hang otherwise undocumented works—especially when they depict a sitter who seems to be recognizably of color. On one occasion, at the time of the landmark 1983 survey exhibition *Painting in the South*, a circa 1840 portrait titled *Slave or Servant of the Douglas Family* (fig. 66) was attributed to him. The curators justified the "possible" attribution of the portrait to Hudson on the basis of "[t]he subject and the placement of the sitter's head in relation to the plain background."[99] However, comparison of the portrait with Hudson's other works suggests that the subject's skin tone, rather than the composition, was the impetus for the attribution.

Figure 64
PORTRAIT OF A WOMAN THOUGHT TO BE
MARIE AGNES POISSOT METOYER
by an unknown artist
ca. 1830s, oil on canvas
courtesy of the Cammie G. Henry Research Center, Watson Library,
Northwestern State University of Louisiana

Figure 65
PRE-TREATMENT PHOTOPRINT OF PORTRAIT OF A WOMAN THOUGHT TO BE
MARIE AGNES POISSOT METOYER
by Lyle Saxon
ca. 1925, photoprint
courtesy of Cammie G. Henry Research Center, Watson Library,
Northwestern State University of Louisiana

Figure 66
SLAVE OR SERVANT OF THE DOUGLAS FAMILY
by an unknown artist
ca. 1850, oil on canvas
courtesy of the Collections of Louisiana State Museum, 11943.54

Figure 67
PORTRAIT OF A YOUNG GENTLEMAN,
THOUGHT TO BE A NEW ORLEANS FREE MAN OF COLOR
by an unknown artist
after 1830, oil on canvas
courtesy of Glynne Couvillion

The practice has been even more frequent on the art market. Recently, a New Orleans auction house sold a small portrait of a young man of color (fig. 67), ascribing the maker to the circle of Julien Hudson or Jules Lion. While the work's handling is sketchier and looser than any extant painted example either artist ever made, it may have seemed a promising sales device to assume that a sitter of color would have been painted by an artist of color. This, of course, ignores the historical evidence mentioned earlier of the plentiful existence of portraits of people of color executed by white artists.

Unlike these previous two examples, the possibility of accurate attributions of other paintings to Hudson is still open to discussion. While the authenticity of the Dallas painting (fig. 10) and the private collection miniature (fig. 8) attributed to Hudson are still in question, their attributions and affinities are rooted more in stylistic characteristics than in markers of racial difference. What the ongoing assignment of works to Hudson's oeuvre means, of course, is that he has become a name to include in exhibitions and auction catalogues, a fact witnessed by the frequency with which *Portrait of a Man* has been borrowed as a self-portrait and by these recent sales.

The search for Hudson is in fact two explorations, both of which raise more questions than they answer. As we have seen, the gaps in the historical record and lack of plentiful signed works make it difficult to successfully resurrect and interpret his career as an artist. The absence of detailed provenances for his work is also difficult to surmount, since it limits our understanding of his patrons and, indeed, their potential stories. Portraiture is a web that often depends upon networks, referrals, and personal relationships. This is particularly true in the study of Louisiana art, where artists and patrons have historically been rather tightly linked.[100]

The other—and more emotionally and politically invested—search is the understanding of Hudson as an artist of color. As we have seen, the artistic and cultural histories of the twentieth and twenty-first centuries have foregrounded at least one part of Hudson's racial mixture to claim a place for him as an important player in African American art. While it is undeniably true that he is the second-earliest securely documented visual artist of African descent in our country's history, his racial identity, and thus his difference from the supposed norm of the white artistic class, can only be located in his heredity, not in the artworks themselves. As we have seen, Hudson's paintings fully participate and share in the dominant artistic conventions of their day—to the extent that Hudson twice sought training at the geographical source of that style. A postcolonial interpretation might be to assume that Hudson had no other choice: that institutionalized racism so affected his and his colleagues' constructions of selves that they had no option but to bend to pressure, deny part of their heritages, and subscribe to the dominant culture. And with hindsight, that might be true—in some respects. But the visual reality is not that simple. There is no apparent difference between Hudson and his colleagues of color's works and that of supposedly all-white artists. The history of Louisiana art is overwhelmingly one of artistic exchange with France—an exchange that built upon conversations among artists of all racial combinations. For that matter, the presence of African motifs in the ironwork of the city's architectural decorations rejects an assumption that any style that could be recognized as having African influences would have been unwelcome in the city where Hudson lived, worked, and died. Likewise, Louisiana's own cuisine—like its art, one of its most distinctive legacies—draws from a combination of cultural traditions.[101] The story of Hudson, then, like the story of race itself in our country, is a complicated one, much more nuanced than any simple opposition or combination of white versus black—and more compelling, for all that.

The search for Hudson reaffirms the primacy of portrait-making to antebellum Louisiana, among artists and sitters of all nationalities and racial compositions. It reminds us of the possibilities and limits of both the archive and the art of connoisseurship. One surety emerges: the role of desire. For it is the viewer's desire to know the story—to fill in the gaps—that propels us across time to connect with the painted world and those who made it and were made by it.

NOTES

1   Patricia Brady, "A Mixed Palette: Free Artists of Color of Antebellum New Orleans," *International Review of African American Art* 12, no. 3 (1995): 5–57.

2   Isaac M. Cline, "Art and Artists in New Orleans Since Colonial Times: A Preliminary Sketch," *Louisiana State Museum Biennial Report of the Board of Curators for 1920–21* (New Orleans: Louisiana State Museum, 1922).

3   See, for example, Margo Preston Moscou, "New Orleans's Freemen of Color: A Forgotten Generation of Cabinetmakers Rediscovered," *Magazine Antiques* 171, no. 5 (2007): 146–53, expanded in book form as *New Orleans' Free-Men-of-Color Cabinet Makers in the New Orleans Furniture Trade, 1800–1850* (New Orleans: Xavier Review Press, 2008).

4   For the most thorough surveys to date, see Patricia Brady, "Black Artists in Antebellum New Orleans," *Louisiana History* 32, no. 1 (1991): 5–28; Brady, "A Mixed Palette," 5–57. See also, on individual artists, Patricia Brady, "Florville Foy, F.M.C.: Master Marble Cutter and Tomb Builder," *Southern Quarterly* 31 (1993): 8–20; Charles East, "Jules Lion's New Orleans," *Georgia Review* 40, no. 4 (1986): 913–52; and Patricia Brady, "Jules Lion, F.M.C: Lithographer Extraordinaire," in *Printmaking in New Orleans*, ed. Jessie J. Poesch (New Orleans: The Historic New Orleans Collection, 2006), 160–75. In addition, a dissertation on Jules Lion is currently in preparation by Sara Mandel Picard for Indiana University. Although this essay concentrates on the contributions of free people of color to the visual culture of New Orleans, a substantial community of free people of color enriched literary and musical culture, as well. See, for example, Dana Kress, "Pierre-Aristide Desdunes, *Les Cenelles*, and the Challenge of Nineteenth-Century Creole Literature," *Southern Quarterly* 44, no. 3 (2007): 42–67; and Bill Marshall, "New Orleans, Nodal Point of the French Atlantic," *International Journal of Francophone Studies* 10, nos. 1–2 (2007): 35–50. The most complete treatment has been Chris Michaelides, *Paroles d'honneur: Ecrits de Créoles de couleur néo-orléanais, 1837–1872* (Shreveport, LA: Editions Tintamarre, 2004). For music, see Lester Sullivan, "Composers of Color of Nineteenth-Century New Orleans," in *Creole: The History and Legacy of Louisiana's Free People of Color*, ed. Sybil Kein (Baton Rouge: Louisiana State University Press, 2000), 71–100.

5   Dragon's race is omitted from John Burton Harter and Mary Louise Tucker, *The Louisiana Portrait Gallery*, vol. 1, *To 1870* (New Orleans: Louisiana State Museum, 1979), no. 9, 20; and Mrs. Thomas Nelson Carter Brun, comp., *Louisiana Portraits* (New Orleans: National Society of the Colonial Dames of America in the State of Louisiana, 1975), 85.

6   For the most recent discussions on Meucci, see Tony Lewis, "Portrait Miniatures at the Louisiana State Museum," *Louisiana Cultural Vistas* 18, no. 1 (2007): 48–51. I am grateful to Dr. Lewis for sharing his manuscript on the Meuccis, which will be included in the *New Encyclopedia of American Folk Art* (University of Mississippi Press, forthcoming).

7   Wendy J. Shadwell and Robert Strunsky, *Catalogue of American Portraits in The New-York Historical Society* (New Haven, CT, and London: Yale University Press, 1974), 2: 804–5.

8   He advertised at least ten times in a short span over the winter of 1826–27, in several newspapers. See "Meucci, Anthony" in *Encyclopædia of New Orleans Artists, 1718–1918*, ed. John A. Mahé II, Rosanne McCaffrey, and Patricia Brady Schmit (New Orleans: The Historic New Orleans Collection, 1987), 261.

9   For an excellent discussion of the history of American portrait miniatures, particularly their making and techniques, see Robin Jaffee Frank, *Love and Loss: American Portrait and Mourning Miniatures*, exh. cat. (New Haven, CT: Yale University Art Gallery, 2000), especially 2–3 and 8–10.

10   Mary Gehman, *The Free People of Color of New Orleans: An Introduction* (New Orleans: Margaret Media, 1994), 53; Doris Dorcas Carter, "Michel Seligny," in *A Dictionary of Louisiana Biography,* ed. Glenn R. Conrad (New Orleans: Louisiana Historical Association, 1988), 2: 732.

11   Michel Fabre, "New Orleans Creole Expatriates in France: Romance and Reality," in *Creole: The History and Legacy*, 179–95.

12   Rodolphe Lucien Desdunes, *Nos hommes et notre histoire* (Montreal: Arbour & Dupont, 1911). All citations from this source will be taken from the translated edition, *Our People and Our History: Fifty Creole Portraits*, trans. Sister Dorothea Olga McCants (Baton Rouge: Louisiana State University Press, 1973).

13   Ibid., 35.

14   Fabre, "New Orleans Creole Expatriates," 182.

15   Bruno Foucart, Geneviève Capy, and G-Florent Laballe, *Guillaume Guillon Lethière, peintre d'histoire, 1760–1832*, exh. cat. (Paris: Suisse Imprimerie, 1991), 7.

16   Simon Lee, "Guillaume Lethière," in *From David to Ingres: Early 19th-Century French Artists*, ed. Jane Turner (New York: St. Martin's Press, 2000), 302–4; Shelby T. McCloy, *The Negro in France* (Lexington: University of Kentucky Press, 1961), 120–21.

17   McCloy, *The Negro in France,* 9, 21–27. See also Ben Melvin Hobratsch, "Creole Angel: The Self-Identity of the Free People of Color of Antebellum New Orleans" (MA thesis, University of North Texas, 2006), 16–18. For a brief survey of nineteenth-century American artists of color in Paris, see Theresa Leininger-Miller, *New Negro Artists in Paris: African American Painters and Sculptors in the City of Light, 1922–1934* (New Brunswick, NJ: Rutgers University Press, 2001). Although the focus of the study is modernism, Leininger-Miller provides a useful survey of the early history of African American art in chapter 1, 1–5. See also Shirley Elizabeth Thompson, "The Passing of a People: Creoles of Color in Mid-Nineteenth Century New Orleans" (PhD diss., Harvard University, 2001), 80–82.

18   Lee, "Guillaume Lethière," 303.

19   Margaret A. Oppenheimer, *The French Portrait: Revolution to Restoration*, exh. cat. (Northampton, MA: Smith College Museum of Art, 2005), 143. Oppenheimer reads portrait likenesses of Lethière as revealing him to be "not obviously mulatto. Judging by contemporary portraits, he had light skin and curly reddish brown hair." This differs from the assessment of the curators of the 1991 Lethière retrospective, who claimed that "Il a les traits fins et les cheveux frisés qui lui donnent ce port altier qui caractérise souvent les enfants nés aux Antilles de deux communautés différentes." [He has the fine features and curly hair that give him the distinct look so common to Caribbean-born children who are the product of two different backgrounds.] See Foucart et al., *Guillaume Guillon Lethière,* 8.

20   Brady, "A Mixed Palette," 7.

21   In August 1831, Hudson applied for a passport to sail from Le Havre, France, to Liverpool, England. One wonders if he left France in search of his father, who disappeared from New Orleans sometime after the 1815 birth of Julien's brother John Joseph. Registre des passeports, 1831, F7*2565, 207, Archives nationales de France, Paris.

22   *Louisiana Courier*, 3 December 1831, 3, c. 4; reprinted in *Louisiana Courier*, 10 January 1832, 3, c. 5. Indeed, although the French version of the advertisement, published in the French edition of the paper three days earlier, does not contain a separate headline, the emphasis on the artist's chosen format is still there. *Courrier de la Louisiane*, 7 January 1832.

23   On Vaudechamp, see William Keyse Rudolph, *Vaudechamp in New Orleans* (New Orleans: The Historic New Orleans Collection, 2007), as well as William Keyse Rudolph, "Jean-Joseph Vaudechamp in France and Louisiana,

1790–1864" (PhD diss., Bryn Mawr College, 2003). Vaudechamp's arrival date is documented in Rudolph, *Vaudechamp in New Orleans*, 103n36.

24 George Coulon, "Old Painters of New Orleans," unpublished MS, 1901, 2, Scrapbook 100, Louisiana State Museum. Coulon's manuscript is the sole written evidence for Fleischbein's presence in Girodet's studio, which cannot be verified in the records of the École nationale supérieure des beaux-arts. No complete record, however, exists of Girodet's pupils. Given Fleischbein's documented relationship with Vaudechamp, it is likely that he indeed was one of Girodet's pupils. Thus, although Coulon's reminiscences of the New Orleans artists of the previous generation contain several inaccuracies, it is likely that in this case he can be trusted. Besides the visual evidence of his sketchbook, Fleischbein's French residency is also confirmed by the personal circumstance of his marriage to Marie Louise (also known as Marie Elise) Têtu, the daughter of a Napoleonic soldier.

25 See George Jordan, "Old Sketch Books Recall Early N.O. Artist," *Times-Picayune*, 4 April 1976, sec. 2, p. 2.

26 [F. Fleischbein, portrait painter, newly arrived from France, has the honor of announcing to the city's inhabitants that he makes all sizes of oil and drawn portraits, guaranteed to be perfect resemblances. Individuals interested in seeing his work and in being painted should present themselves at the Hotel de la Marine on Levee Street.] *L'Abeille*, 8 June 1833, 3, c. 4.

27 Randolph Delehanty, *Art in the American South: Works in the Ogden Collection* (Baton Rouge: Louisiana State University Press, 1996), 187.

28 On Abel de Pujol, see Isabelle Denis, "Abel de Pujol, Alexandre," in *From David to Ingres*, ed. Turner, 1–2. For the Legrand portrait, see *Forgotten French Art from the First to the Second Empire*, exh. cat. (London: Heim Gallery, 1978), n.p., no. 14.

29 On the close emotional ties of the members of the Davidian school, see Thomas E. Crow, *Emulation: Making Artists for Revolutionary France* (New Haven, CT: Yale University Press, 1995).

30 AJ52*246–248, AJ52*553, AJ52*926, Archives Nationales de France, Coupas to Rudolph, 3 October 2008, 3–4; P30 Abel de Pujol, Archives des Musées Nationaux.

31 Coupas to Rudolph, 2–3.

32 Coupas to Rudolph, 2.

33 Passenger Lists of Vessels Arriving at New York, New York, 1820–1897 (National Archives Microfilm Publication M237, roll 34); Records of the U.S. Customs Service, Record Group 36; National Archives, Washington, DC.

34 Ancestry.com, New Orleans, Louisiana Death Records Index, 1804–1949 [database online] (Provo, UT: The Generations Network, Inc., 2002), 6: 60. See also Brady, "A Mixed Palette," 6.

35 Ancestry.com, New Orleans, Lousiana Death Records Index, 1804–1949, 6: 132.

36 Neal Auction Company, "New Orleans, Louisiana Purchase Auction," September 30 and October 1, 2006, lot 333; repr. 66.

37 Christian Alcindor, "Les Gens de couleur libres de la Nouvelle-Orléans, 1803–1865: Leur rang social dans la société esclavagiste" (MA thesis, Université de Montréal, 1995), 37–46; Laura Foner, "The Free People of Color in Louisiana and St. Dominigue: A Comparative Portrait of Two Three-Caste Slave Societies," *Journal of Social History* 3 (1970): 427–29; Moscou, "New Orleans's Freemen of Color," 152.

38 See Roger A. Fischer, "Racial Segregation in Ante Bellum New Orleans," *The American Historical Review* 74, no. 3 (1969): 926–37, especially 935–37.

39 George Coulon, "Old Painters of New Orleans," 2. For discussion of the manuscript, see Judith Hopkins Bonner, "George David Coulon: A Nineteenth Century French Louisiana Painter," *Southern Quarterly* 20, no. 2 (1982): 42, 59.

40 Coulon, "Old Painters of New Orleans," 1.

41 Ibid., 2.

42 Bonner, "George David Coulon," 42. For Bonner's comparative discussion of Coulon's *Boy with a Rose* and Hudson's *Creole Boy with a Moth* and *Portrait of a Young Girl with a Rose*, see 45–47.

43 Mrs. A. G. Durno, "Art," in *Standard History of New Orleans, Louisiana*, ed. Henry Rightor (Chicago: Lewis Publishing Company, 1900), 381.

44 Durno's text also contains multiple factual errors. See Brady, "Black Artists in Antebellum New Orleans," 9.

45 Desdunes, *Our People and Our History*, 71.

46 See, for example, W. E. B. DuBois, "Free Negroes of Louisiana," in *Black Reconstruction in America* (New York: Atheneum, 1935), 154–55. See also the more recent survey of African American art in New Orleans by Harriet JoAnne Walker, "A Feminist Study of African American Art in New Orleans: Considerations of Aesthetics, Art History and Criticism" (PhD diss., Louisiana State University, 1997), 227.

47 John Smith Kendall, *History of New Orleans* (Chicago and New York: Lewis Publishing, 1922), 2: 656.

48 Cline, "Art and Artists in New Orleans," 32–42.

49 *Louisiana State Museum Biennial Report of the Board of Curators for 1920–21* (New Orleans: Louisiana State Museum, 1922): 65.

50 Cline, "Art and Artists in New Orleans," 33.

51 On Cline, see Mrs. Peter Thompson, "Isaac Monroe Cline," in *Dictionary of Louisiana Biography*, 1: 186–87.

52 Ben Earl Looney, "Historical Sketch of Art in Louisiana," *Louisiana Historical Quarterly* 18, no. 1 (1935): 389.

53 *Louisiana State Museum Biennial Report*, 65.

54 Robert Glenk, *Louisiana State Museum: Handbook of Information Concerning its Historic Buildings and the Treasures They Contain* (New Orleans: Louisiana State Museum, 1934), 76.

55 Ethel Hutson, "Isaac Delgado Museum of Art," *Warrington Messenger* (New Orleans), September 1938, 19. Note that in addition to substituting "Jules" for Julien, Hutson also incorrectly stated the date of Julien Hudson's studies in Paris.

56 Brady, "Black Artists in Antebellum New Orleans," 8.

57 Ibid.

58 James A. Porter, *Modern Negro Art* (Washington, DC: Howard University Press, 1992; orig. publ. 1943), 37–38; Arna Bontemps, *Story of the Negro* (New York: Alfred A. Knopf, 1948), 119. See also Edward Strickland, "Our 'Forgotten' Negro Artists," *Masses & Mainstream* 7 (September 1954): 34–40, which discusses Hudson on 38–39, listing the two Louisiana State Museum portraits but getting his decade of activity in New Orleans wrong.

59 Cedric Dover, *American Negro Art* (New York: New York Graphic Society, 1960), 21.

60 For example, Theresa Dickason Cederholm, *Afro-American Artists: A Bio-bibliographical Directory* (Boston: Boston Public Library, 1973), 134; Elsa Honig Fine, *The Afro American Artist: A Search for Identity* (New York: Holt, Rinehart and Winston, 1973), 30; as well as Janet E. Taylor, *Black Art: Reviewing Its Roots* (Ann Arbor, MI: Tay-Pick Co. and Black Vibrations Publishing, 1972), n.p.

61 James A. Porter, *Ten Afro-American Artists of the Nineteenth Century: An Exhibition Commemorating the Centennial of Howard University*, exh. cat. (Washington, DC: Gallery of Art, Howard University, 1967), 16–17, with text that is virtually the same as Porter's 1943 discussion of Hudson; Jehanne Teilhet, *Dimensions of Black*, exh. cat. (La Jolla, CA: La Jolla Museum of Art, 1970), 64, 66, no. 167; Ann C. Van Deventer and Alfred V. Frankenstein, *American Self-Portraits, 1670–1973*, exh. cat. (Washington, DC: International Exhibitions Foundation, 1974), no. 23, 60–61; David C. Driskell with Leonard Simon, *Two Centuries of Black American Art*, exh. cat. (New York: Alfred A. Knopf and Los Angeles County Museum of Art, 1976), no. 23, 122; and Regenia A. Perry, *Selections of Nineteenth-Century Afro-American Art*, exh. cat. (New York: Metropolitan Museum of Art, 1976), n.p.

62 Perry, *Selections of Nineteenth-Century Afro-American Art*, n.p.

63 Samella Lewis, *African American Art and Artists*, updated and rev. ed. (Berkeley and Los Angeles: University of California Press, 1990; orig. publ. 1978), 15.

64 Gwendolyn DuBois Shaw, *Portraits of a People: Picturing African Americans in the Nineteenth Century*, exh. cat. (Andover, MA: Addison Gallery of American Art, 2006), 84, 86.

65 The literature is rapidly growing, but as representative examples, see Richard Brilliant, *Portraiture* (Cambridge, MA: Harvard University Press, 1991); Harry Berger, *Fictions of the Pose: Rembrandt Against the Italian Renaissance* (Stanford, CA: Stanford University Press, 2000); and Shearer West, *Portraiture* (Oxford: Oxford University Press, 2004).

66   As Charles Edwards O'Neill wrote in 1979, "Traditional attribution holds that the portrait [at the LSM] is a self-portrait; clear proof is not available." See O'Neill, "Fine Arts and Literature: Nineteenth-Century Louisiana Black Artists and Authors," in *Louisiana's Black Heritage*, ed. Robert R. Macdonald, John R. Kemp, and Edward F. Haas (New Orleans: Louisiana State Museum, 1979): 63–84; quotation from 73n28. Patricia Brady also pointed out the lack of conclusive evidence, as mentioned above, in Brady, "Black Artists in Antebellum New Orleans," 8–9, and Brady, "A Mixed Palette," 8.

67   See, for example, A. D. Macklin, *A Biographical History of African-American Artists, A–Z* (Lewiston, NY: Edwin Mellen Press, 2001), 39, which lists Hudson's birthdate as around 1830, among other errors; Dennis Thomison, comp., *The Black Artist in America: An Index to Reproductions* (Metuchen, NJ: Scarecrow Press, 1991), 138.

68   The difficulty in a facile diagnosis of African echoes in Louisiana art operates in distinct difference to the easier identification of the continuation of African cultural and aesthetic traditions in the art of enslaved people in other regions of the South, such as in the patterning of quilts and the stylized features of face jars. On plantation arts, see, for example, Sharon F. Patton, *African American Art* (Oxford: Oxford University Press, 1998), 34–38.

69   *Les Cenelles* is generally recognized as the first anthology of poetry published in the United States by individuals of African descent. For a recent discussion of *Les Cenelles*, see Shirley Elizabeth Thompson, *Exiles at Home: The Struggle to Become American in Creole New Orleans* (Cambridge: Harvard University Press, 2009), 117–18, 126–29, and 308n17.

70   See Brady, "Black Artists in Antebellum New Orleans," 20–24, and Brady, "A Mixed Palette," 13–14, 53–54.

71   Warburg was apparently commissioned to work on a now-lost set of sculptural reliefs that explicitly referenced the African American condition by illustrating Harriet Beecher Stowe's *Uncle Tom's Cabin*. However, these were commissioned by a white Englishwoman, not done on speculation.

72   "Antrobus, John," in *Encyclopædia of New Orleans Artists*, 10–11; Judith H. Bonner, "Paintings from the Permanent Collection of The Historic New Orleans Collection" in Patricia Brady et al., *Complementary Visions of Louisiana Art: The Laura Simon Nelson Collection at The Historic New Orleans Collection* (New Orleans: The Historic New Orleans Collection, 1996), 68.

73   After the Civil War, of course, the sentimental, retroactive plantation paintings of happy, industrious slaves by artists such as William Aiken Walker and August Norieri flourished. William H. Gerdts, "Louisiana Art: Regionally Unique; Southern Exemplar," in *Complementary Visions*, 22; George E. Jordan, "The Laura Simon Nelson Collection, 1840s–1970s," in *Complementary Visions*, 42–43; Estill Curtis Pennington, *Downriver: Currents of Style in Louisiana Painting, 1800–1950* (Gretna, LA: Pelican Publishing Company, 1991), especially chapter 5, "The Black Image in Louisiana Painting," 109–24.

74   My thanks to Carrie Rebora Barratt of the Metropolitan Museum of Art for identifying the hairstyle and tracing its appearance across American portraiture.

75   Harter and Tucker, *Louisiana Portrait Gallery*, 20; Brun, *Louisiana Portraits*, 85.

76   For extended discussion, see Thompson, *Exiles at Home*, 27–30, 38–66.

77   See Shaw, *Portraits of a People*, 72–74.

78   Hobratsch details these patterns in "Creole Angel," 32–48.

79   Desdunes, *Our People and Our History*, 3.

80   On Johnson, see J. Hall Pleasants, *Joshua Johnston, the First American Negro Portrait Painter* (Baltimore: Maryland Historical Society, 1942); Carolyn J. Weekley, et. al., *Joshua Johnson: Freeman and Early American Portrait Painter*, exh. cat. (Williamsburg, VA, and Baltimore, MD: Abby Aldrich Rockefeller Folk Art Center and Maryland Historical Society, 1987).

81   George William Featherstonhaugh, *Excursions Through the Slave States* (New York: Harper & Brothers, 1847), 141.

82   Shaw reproduces and discusses these; see *Portraits of a People*, 152–61.

83   Brady, "Black Artists in Antebellum New Orleans," 8n7.

84   Brady, "A Mixed Palette," 8; 56n9.

85   For *Creole Boy*, see Sotheby's New York, "Important Americana: Silver, Porcelain, Prints, Folk Art and Furniture," sale 7420, January 21–22, 2000, lot 482, repr. 210. For the *Gentleman*, see Brady, "A Mixed Palette," 7.

86   The classic text on the Metoyers remains Gary B. Mills, *The Forgotten People: Cane River's Creoles of Color* (Baton Rouge: Louisiana State University Press, 1977). See also Elizabeth Shown Mills and Gary B. Mills, "The Louisiana Metoyers: Melrose's Story of Land and Slaves," *American Visions* 15, no. 3 (2000): 40–41; condensed from "Slaves and Masters: The Louisiana Metoyers," *National Genealogical Society Quarterly* 70 (1982): 164–89. For a recent overview of the historical background, see H. Sophie Burton and F. Todd Smith, *Colonial Natchitoches: A Creole Community on the Louisiana-Texas Frontier* (College Station: Texas A & M University Press, 2008), especially chapter 4, "Free People of Color: A Dependent Segment of Colonial Natchitoches," 88–104. See also Elizabeth Shown Mills, "*Isle of Canes* and Issues of Conscience: Master-Slave Sexual Dynamics and Slaveholding by Free People of Color," *Southern Quarterly* 43, no. 2 (2006): 158–75, which speculatively revisits the topic after many years of reflection and research. For a carefully nuanced discussion of the multiple histories of Melrose, see David W. Morgan, Kevin C. MacDonald, and Fiona J. L. Handley, "Economics and Authenticity: A Collision of Interpretations in Cane River National Heritage Area, Louisiana," *George Wright Forum* 23, no. 1 (2006): 44–62.

87   Melrose's strongest artistic legacy, incidentally, was not the works of many of the white painters and writers associated with it, but rather—and rather ironically—the oeuvre of its African American cook and housekeeper, the self-taught artist Clementine Hunter (1887–1988), who has become an icon of self-taught painting.

88   See, for example, Lyle Saxon, "Easter Sunday at Aunt Cammie's," *Times-Picayune* Magazine Section, Sunday, April 22, 1923, 1, complete with devoted African American servants speaking in dialect.

89   Morgan et al., "Economics and Authenticity," 49, 52–53. Representative examples of Mignon's style can be found throughout his papers; see for example a brief history of Melrose written in 1971, "Cane River Memo," François Mignon Papers, 3889, folder 584, frame 311.

90   See Judith Wilson, "Optical Illusions: Images of Miscegenation in Nineteenth- and Twentieth-Century Art," *American Art* 5, no. 3 (1991): 89–107, for the portrait, 92; also Shaw, *Portraits of a People*, 84. For a discussion of the sitters' identities and the work's provenance, see George Jordan, "Mystery Surrounds Louisiana Painting in Met Exhibit," and response by Alberta Collier, *Times-Picayune,* 25 July 1976, sec. 2, p. 2.

91   A question raised by Brady, "A Mixed Palette," 11 and 57n21.

92   Melrose Collection, folder 1441, 5-B-4, Lyle Saxon's Album, Cammie G. Henry Research Center, Watson Library, Northwestern State University, Natchitoches, Louisiana.

93   The portrait thought to depict Agnes Poissot Metoyer was donated to the Center by the Henry family in 1980, after having been on loan since 1970. Curatorial file, Henry Research Center, Watson Library, Northwestern State University.

94   François Mignon Collection, folder 104, Henry Research Library.

95   Elizabeth Shown Mills to author, email communication, September 10, 2009.

96   Elizabeth Shown Mills to author, email communication, September 11, 2009. I am also very grateful to Kathleen Balthazar, compiler of the massive Cane River families' genealogies, for her assistance.

97   Mary Linn Wernet to author, email communication, November 29, 2006; Elizabeth Shown Mills to author, email communication, September 11, 2009.

98   François Mignon, typewritten MS, "Yucca House, Melrose Plantation, Melrose," Mignon Papers, UNC, folder 596, frame 695, accessed at Henry Research Center, Northwestern University, Natchitoches, Louisiana.

99   Ella Price-Knox, et al., *Painting in the South: 1564–1980*, exh. cat. (Richmond, VA: Virginia Museum, 1983), 262, cat. 67.

100 Discussed in detail by William Keyse Rudolph, "Uniting Creole Families Through Art," keynote address, Creole History Day, Louisiana Historical Society, The Historic New Orleans Collection, 26 October 2007.

101 On New Orleans ironwork, see Eva Regina Martin, "Forging from Sunup to Sundown: African Symbols in the Works of Black Ironworkers in New Orleans (1800–1863)" (PhD diss., Temple University, 1995), as well as Walker, "A Feminist Study of African American Art in New Orleans," 218–22.

EXHIBITION CHECKLIST

Nicholas Legrand and His Grandson,
Joseph-Adolphe de Pujol
by Alexandre-Denis Abel de Pujol
1815, oil on canvas, 45 x 38"
courtesy of the High Museum, purchased with funds
from the Phoenix Society and purchased with funds
given by Alfred Austell Thornton in memory of
Leila Austell Thornton and Albert Edward
Thornton Sr., and Sarah Miller Venable and
William Hoyt Venable, 1990.2

Carl Kohn
by Jacques Guillaume Lucien Amans
ca. 1837, oil on canvas, 36 1/4 x 28 1/2"
The Historic New Orleans Collection, 2006.0425.1

A Digest of the Ordinances, By-laws, and
Regulations of the Corporation of New Orleans*
by the New Orleans City Council
New Orleans: Gaston Bruslé, 1836
The Historic New Orleans Collection, 76-738-RL

Portrait of a Free Woman of Color
by Louis-Antoine Collas
1829, oil on canvas, 38 3/4 x 31"
courtesy of the New Orleans Museum of Art,
gift of Dr. I. M. Cline, 38.1

Boy with a Rose
by George David Coulon
1842, oil on canvas, 22 x 18"
courtesy of the Collections of Louisiana State Museum,
04931

Nos hommes et notre histoire*
by Rodolphe Lucien Desdunes
Montreal: Arbour & Dupont, 1911
The Historic New Orleans Collection, 69-201-LP.5

Marie Louise Têtu, Madame François Fleischbein
by François (Franz) Fleischbein
ca. 1833–36, oil on canvas, 6 x 7 1/4"
courtesy of the Dallas Museum of Art, gift of
the Patsy Lacy Griffith Collection, by exchange,
and the American Painting Fund

Portrait of a Creole Lady
by François (Franz) Fleischbein
ca. 1830s, oil on canvas, 44 1/2 x 71 3/4"
courtesy of Matilda Gray Stream

Portrait of Betsy
by François (Franz) Fleischbein
1837, oil on canvas, 28 1/4 x 22 1/4"
The Historic New Orleans Collection, 1985.212

Child with Drum
by Florville Foy
ca. 1838, marble
*courtesy of the Collections of Louisiana State Museum,
gift of M. Marcell, 00216*

*Gibson's Guide and Directory of the
State of Louisiana, and the Cities of New Orleans
and Lafayette**
New Orleans: John Gibson, 1838
The Historic New Orleans Collection, 87-085-RL

Portrait of a Young Girl with a Rose
by Julien Hudson
1834, oil on canvas, 16 1/4 x 13 1/4"
courtesy of the Zigler Museum

Creole Boy with a Moth
by Julien Hudson
1835, oil on canvas, 29 x 23"
courtesy of a private collection

Portrait of a Black Man
by Julien Hudson
1835, oil on canvas, 30 1/4 x 25 1/8"
courtesy of a private collection

Jean Michel Fortier
by Julien Hudson
1839, oil on canvas, 30 x 35"
*courtesy of the Collections of Louisiana State Museum,
gift of Marguerite Fortier, 11321*

Portrait of a Man, Called a Self-Portrait
by Julien Hudson
1839, oil on canvas, 8 3/4 x 7"
*courtesy of the Collections of Louisiana State Museum,
07526 B*

Portrait Miniature of a Creole Lady
attributed to Julien Hudson
ca. 1837–39, oil on panel, 7" height
*courtesy of the collection of Laura Schwartz
and Arthur Jussel*

Portrait of a Creole Gentleman
attributed to Julien Hudson
ca. 1835–37, oil on canvas, 13 1/4 x 11"
*courtesy of the Dallas Museum of Art,
gift of Curtis E. Ransom*

Portrait of a Creole Woman of Color
by Aimable-Désiré Lansot
ca. 1845, oil on canvas, 41 1/2 x 34 1/2"
*courtesy of the Collections of Louisiana State Museum,
1993.105*

Les Cenelles: Choix de poésies indigènes
by Armand Lanusse, editor and contributor
New Orleans: H. Lauve, 1845
The Historic New Orleans Collection, 87-632-RL

Villere
by Jules Lion
1837, lithograph, 14 1/8 x 10 5/8"
The Historic New Orleans Collection, 1970.11.41

Eliza Field, Eliza Dubourg Field, and Odile Field
by Jules Lion
1838, lithograph, 14 1/8 x 10 5/8"
The Historic New Orleans Collection, 1970.11.141

André Martin
by Jules Lion
1841, lithograph, 14 1/8 x 10 5/8"
The Historic New Orleans Collection, 1959.13.75

The Cathedral of New Orleans/La Cathédrale
by Jules Lion
1842, lithograph, 18 7/8 x 13 5/8"
*The Historic New Orleans Collection,
bequest of Richard Koch, 1971.32*

Achille Lion
by Jules Lion
between 1837 and 1847, lithograph, 14 1/8 x 10 5/8"
The Historic New Orleans Collection, 1970.11.22

Marius S. Bringier
by Jules Lion
between 1837 and 1847, lithograph, 14 1/8 x 10 5/8"
The Historic New Orleans Collection, 1959.13.2

*Letter from Jules Lion to the members of the
construction committee of the St. Louis Cathedral**
by Jules Lion
December 8, 1850
*The Historic New Orleans Collection,
gift of Samuel Wilson Jr., 86-74-L.2*

Creole Woman Accompanied by Confederate Symbols
attributed to Arthur Lumley
ca. 1861, watercolor, 29 1/2 x 24 1/2"
courtesy of a private collection

Dona Maria Theresa Piconelle
by Antonio Meucci
ca. 1818, watercolor on ivory, 3 1/4 x 2 5/8"
*courtesy of the Collections of Louisiana State Museum,
08943.30*

Portrait of a Gentleman
by Antonio Meucci
ca. 1825, watercolor on ivory, 3" diameter
*courtesy of the New Orleans Museum of Art, Museum
Purchase, Shirley Latter Kaufmann Fund, 99.63*

Girl with a Rattle
by Antonio Meucci
ca. 1825, watercolor on ivory, 3 1/4" height
courtesy of a private collection through Elle Shushan

Marianne Celeste Dragon
attributed to the school of José Francisco Xavier de
Salazar y Mendoza
ca. 1795, oil on canvas, 37 1/4 x 30 1/4"
*courtesy of the Collections of Louisiana State Museum,
gift of John T. Block, 05750*

*Acts Passed at the Second Session of the Ninth
Legislature of the State of Louisiana**
by the State of Louisiana
Donaldsonville, La.: C. W. Duhy, 1830
*The Historic New Orleans Collection,
gift of Mrs. Robert C. Hills, 86-35-RL*

*Portrait of a Young Gentleman, Thought
to Be a New Orleans Free Man of Color*
by an unknown artist
after 1830, oil on canvas, 8 3/4 x 6 1/2"
courtesy of Glynne Couvillion

*Portrait of a Lady, Presumed to be
a Free Woman of Color**
by an unknown artist
1857, pastel, gouache, and oil on paper, 27 x 21 1/2"
courtesy of Leah M. Coleman

*Marie Althée Josephine D'Aquin de Puèch
and Ernest Auguste de Puèch*
by Jean-Joseph Vaudechamp
1832, oil on canvas, 36 x 32"
The Historic New Orleans Collection, 2005.0340.1

*Portrait of a Little Girl, called "Euphrosine"**
by Jean-Joseph Vaudechamp
1836, oil on canvas, 36 x 32"
courtesy of a private collection

*Diagram and letter submitted by Eugène Warburg
to the members of the construction committee of the
St. Louis Cathedral*
by Eugène Warburg
February 12, 1851
*The Historic New Orleans Collection,
gift of Samuel Wilson Jr., 86-74-L.1*

John Young Mason
by Eugène Warburg
1855, marble, 23 x 15 x 10"
courtesy of the Virginia Historical Society, 1927.21

* New Orleans venue only

ACKNOWLEDGMENTS

This exhibition is made possible through loans made by the Dallas Museum of Art; High Museum of Art in Atlanta, Georgia; Louisiana State Museum in New Orleans, Louisiana; New Orleans Museum of Art; private collections of Leah M. Coleman, Glynne Couvillion, Laura Schwartz and Arthur Jussel, and Matilda Gray Stream; Virginia Historical Society in Richmond, Virginia; Zigler Art Museum in Jennings, Louisiana; and those lenders who have chosen to remain anonymous.

The Historic New Orleans Collection, Worcester Art Museum, and Gibbes Museum of Art extend special thanks to Don Didier and the members of the *In Search of Julien Hudson* advisory committee, including Jonn E. Hankins, Executive Director of the New Orleans African American Museum, and Maurie D. McInnis, Associate Professor in the McIntire Department of Art at the University of Virginia. This exhibition would not have been possible without their valuable insight and assistance.

The Collection and Worcester Art Museum would also like to acknowledge the contributions of the Eugene McDermott Director Bonnie Pitman and Chair of Collections and Exhibitions Tamara Wootton-Bonner at the Dallas Museum of Art, under whose auspices this exhibition originated. Initial research support was provided by the Terra Foundation for American Art.

WORCESTER ART MUSEUM

James A. Welu, *Director*
William Keyse Rudolph, *Curator of American Art*
Kate E. Dalton, *Curatorial Assistant*
Deborah Diemente, *Senior Registrar*
Rita Albertson, *Chief Conservator*
Birgit Straehle, *Fellow in Paintings Conservation*
Honee A. Hess, *Director of Education*
Patrick Brown, *Exhibition Designer and Chief Preparator*
Anne Greene, John Hyden, and Trevor Toney, *Preparators*

GIBBES MUSEUM OF ART

Angela D. Mack, *Executive Director and Chief Curator*
Sara Arnold, *Associate Curator of Collections*
Pam S. Wall, *Associate Curator of Exhibitions and Interpretation*
Zinnia Willits, *Collections Manager*

**NATIONAL
ENDOWMENT
FOR THE ARTS**

This project is supported in part by an award from the National Endowment for the Arts.

INDEX